After The Collision: “Abandon The Ship

European University Studies

Europäische Hochschulschriften
Publications Universitaires Européennes

Series II
Law

Reihe II Série II
Rechtswissenschaft
Law

Vol./Bd. 4538

PETER LANG
Frankfurt am Main · Berlin · Bern · Bruxelles · New York · Oxford · Wien

Harry Stamelos

After The Collision: "Abandon The Ship"

A Comparative Study of UK and Hellenic Marine Insurance Law

PETER LANG
Europäischer Verlag der Wissenschaften

Bibliographic Information published by the Deutsche Nationalbibliothek
The Deutsche Nationalbibliothek lists this publication in the Deutsche Nationalbibliografie; detailed bibliographic data is available in the internet at <http://www.d-nb.de>.

ISSN 0531-7312
ISBN 978-3-631-56424-0

www.peterlang.de

To my sister Maria

FOREWORD

The present monograph has been the result of a thorough analysis of the UK and Hellenic Marine Insurance Law issues, especially relating to collisions of vessels and to abandonment. Of great importance is also the matter of burden and standard of proof in the respective litigation. The text has been rewritten and updated up to January 2007.

ACKNOWLEDGMENTS

I would like to thank Professor Robert Wight, at the University of Essex, Department of Law, who supervised my LL.M. dissertation in the respective study of Marine Insurance Law. His comments were essential and necessary for me to complete with success the comparative study. I also thank for his overall support Professor Nicolaos Scandamis who is currently Supervisor Professor of my PhD at the University of Athens, Department of Law.

CONTENTS

MAIN ABBREVIATIONS

A. English (and German)

AC	Law Reports, Appeal Cases (3rd Series)
All ER	All England Law Reports
App Cas	Law Reports, Appeal Cases (2nd Series)
BGB	Bürgerliches Gesetzbuch (German Civil Code)
CA	Court of Appeal
Ch D	Law Reports, Chancery Division (2nd Series)
CIF	Cost Insurance Freight
Co	Company
Corpn	Corporation
CPD	Law Reports, Common Pleas Division
EC	European Community
EG	Europäische Gemeinschaft
FOB	Free On Board
GmbH	Gesellschaft mit beschränkter Haftung
HL	House of Lords
IMO	International Maritime Organization
Inc	Incorporation
Ins	Insurance
ITCF	Institute Time Clauses Freight
ITCH	Institute Time Clauses Hulls
IVCF	Institute Voyage Clauses Freight
IVCH	Institute Voyage Clauses Hulls
IWSC	Institute War and Strikes Clauses
KB	Law Reports, King's Bench
KBD	King's Bench Division
LJ	Lord Justice (Judge)
LJQB	Law Journal Reports, Queen's Bench New Series
Ll L Rep	Lloyd's List Law Reports
Lloyd's Rep	Lloyd's Law Reports
LMCLQ	Lloyd's Maritime and Commercial Law Quarterly
LR	Law Reports (1st Series)
Ltd	Limited Liability Company
P & I	Protection and Indemnity
PD	Law Reports, Probate, Divorce & Admiralty Division
PPI	Policy Proof of Interest
QB	Law Reports, Queen's Bench (3rd Series)
QBD	Law Reports, Queen's Bench Division
SA	Société Anonyme
StGB	Strafgesetzbuch (German Penal Code)
TEU	Treaty on European Union

TLR	Times Law Reports
UK	United Kingdom of Great Britain and Northern Ireland
US	United States Supreme Court Reports
USA	United States of America
V	Versus
WLR	Weekly Law Reports

For an analytical UK – US list of abbreviations see also Stamelos C., NoB 53 (2005) 1955, [available also on the web page of the Athens Law School]

B. Hellenic

AK	Hellenic Civil Code (Astikos Kodikas)
ΑΠ	Areios Pagos (Hellenic Supreme Court for Civil and Penal Cases)
Δ	Trial (Dike, Periodical)
ΕΕΔ	Review of Commercial Law (Epitheorisi Emporikou Dikaiou)
ΕλλΔικ	Hellenic Justice (Elliniki Dikaiosini, Periodical)
ΕΝΔ	Review of Maritime Law (Epitheorisi Naftikou Dikaiou, Periodical)
ΕπΣυγκΔ	Review of Transport Law (Epitheorisi Syginoniakou Dikaiou)
ΕφΑθ	Athens Court of Appeal (Efeteio Athinon)
ΕφΘεσ	Thessaloniki Court of Appeal (Efeteio Thessalonikis)
ΕφΠειρ	Piraeus Court of Appeal (Efeteio Pireos)
Θ	Justice (Themis, Periodical)
ΚΙΝΔ	Code of Private Maritime Law (Kodikas Idiotikou Naftikou Dikaiou)
ΜΠΑθ	One Member Athens Court of First Instance (Monomeles Protodikeio Athinon)
ΜΠΘεσ	One Member Thessaloniki Court of First Instance (Monomeles Protodikeio Thessalonikis)
ΜΠΠειρ	One Member Piraeus Court of First Instance (Monomeles Protodikeio Pireos)
NoB	Legal Step (Nomiko Vima, Periodical)
ΠΠΑθ	Multi (three) Member Athens Court of First Instance (Polymeles Protodikeio Athinon)
ΠΠΘεσ	Multi (three) Member Thessaloniki Court of First Instance (Polymeles Protodikeio Thessalonikis)
ΠΠΚορ	Multi (three) Member Corinth Court of First Instance (Polymeles Protodikeio Korinthou)
ΠΠΠειρ	Multi (three) Member Piraeus Court of First Instance (Polymeles Protodikeio Pireos)
ΣτΕ	Council of State (Hellenic Supreme Court for Administrative Cases)

Synopsis

First Part

In the First Part, the legal issues relating to collision between vessels or a vessel and an object are examined. For example, if the object is a mine, it is a matter of war risks. In addition, the significance of the Third Parties Rights Act 1930 and of the Sistership and Paramount Clauses is explored.
In this Part, the Hellenic Law and some issues in International Maritime Law are explained. Moreover, the similarities and the differences between the UK and the Hellenic Law are defined. It is analyzed how the one system can affect the other, why they appear to be different.

Second Part

In the Second Part, two main issues are the subject matters of the analysis. First, it is discussed the abandonment and its relationship to constructive total loss. Second, extended reference is made to the notice procedure regarding abandonment. Of course, other legal issues (for example, abandonment and subrogation) are also dealt with.

In this Part, Hellenic Law aspects are mentioned and how they are related to the UK Law. Similar matters as stated in the second paragraph in the First Part above are examined. A statutory model by using the advantages of the two legal systems is presented at the end of the Second Part.

Third Part

In the Third Part we examine the procedural rules mainly in the UK regarding burden and standard of proof, not only in the context of the First and Second Part, but also for claims of marine insurance in general.

PART I
COLLISION

A. General

In this Part we attempt to compare the English and the Hellenic marine insurance law regulating the liability of the underwriter arising from collision[1] of an insured vessel with other vessel or vessels or with other objects. Although there are substantial differences between the two legal systems, it is shown that the two systems are not completely different.

For example, there are differences concerning the concepts 'collision' and 'other vessel' and the three – fourths collision liability of the insurer. However, the insurer's liability against the assured does not extend to sums (paid by the assured) for loss of life or personal injury due to collision under the two legal orders.

Throughout the text there is one other comparison. It regards the legal aspects and the liability of the underwriter in collision between motor vehicles. The fact that collision between vessels and collision between vehicles is a peril insured does not necessarily mean that the underwriter is liable for damages caused to third parties in a similar legal way.

B. Collision with other vessel

a. United Kingdom marine insurance law

Collision with other vessel is an (insurable) peril of the sea[2]. This means that in a collision the underwriter may be liable against the assured for a loss of or damage to the insured vessel or cargo, if the policy specifically covers such peril (collision with other vessel). Even if the master or the crew has been negligent, the insurer is still legally bound[3] to cover the loss of or damage to the subject – matter insured.

---

[1] Deliberately collisions between warships fall outside the scope of the present text. For the relevant issues regarding maritime limits and boundaries, see Soons, and Cushman.

[2] Clause 6 of the Institute Time Clauses Hulls (*ITCH*) states that 'this insurance covers loss of or damage to the subject – matter insured caused by perils of the seas'. Since 1887 (*The Xantho*) it has been ruled that collision is a peril of the sea. Perils of the seas are specified maritime perils. In 1883 (*Woodley*) the Court of Appeal held that only a collision resulting at least in part from the action of the winds or waves could be classified as a peril of the sea. Clauses 24 – 27 (ITCH) are under the Paramount Clause (usually in red ink) which states that the clauses 'shall be paramount and shall override anything in the insurance inconsistent therewith'. The loss of the vessel herself is not recoverable, if the proximate causes are collision and a war risk or other risk described in clauses 24 –27 (ITCH). Proximate cause is a principle of causation (what caused the loss and if the cause is a peril covered by the policy) which is discussed by Bennett (pp. 115 – 135) and it falls outside the scope of the present text.

[3] Section 55(2)a of the Marine Insurance Act 1906 (*the Act*).

If two vessels collide, there are two major categories or types of collision. First, the collision may have been an inevitable accident[4] for which no person or vessel is to blame. Second, the collision may have been the result of human fault; one or both vessels are to blame. Maritime law regulates the degree of blame in collision cases. In the United Kingdom, the Maritime Conventions Act 1911 adopted the Brussels International Collision Convention 1910 regulating the degree of blame in collision cases between vessels[5].

In both types of collision the underwriter is legally bound to cover the loss of or damage to the insured vessel or cargo. In cargo insurance, this is provided under the Institute Cargo Clauses (B) and (C), clause 1.1.4.. The distinction between categories of collision becomes vital important in the context of the liability of the underwriter against damages paid by the assured to third parties. This is discussed in the next Chapter.

The question in this Chapter is twofold. What exactly does collision mean in marine insurance terms? First, this question relates to what the policies cover for loss of or damage to the subject – matter insured. Second, this question also relates to the next Chapter: what clause 8 of the Institute Time Clauses Hulls (the collision liability clause) includes in the term 'collision with other vessel'. If clause 8 is decided that it covers the *x* case, then the insurer becomes liable under this clause and such liability (concept, prerequisites and legal consequences) is discussed in the next Chapter.

First, collision as an insured peril of the sea means collision or contact of an insured vessel with land conveyance, dock or harbour equipment or installation,

---

[4] Article 2 of the Brussels International Collision Convention 1910 (*the Brussels Convention*) regulates in the same way (*each party is liable for its damages*) collisions caused by *force majeure* or collisions the causes of which remain in doubt. In s h i p p i n g casualties, *inevitable accident*, when it occurs, is often either the result of extremes of weather or of unexpected mechanical failure as Grime (p. 165) mentions. Grime (p. 166) argues that 'the defence of inevitable accident is never an easy argument to mount'. In *The Virginia Dollar*, however, it was shown that a steel bollard on the wharf had broken before Virginia Dollar colliding with Storborg damaging her. The owners of the Virginia Dollar succeeded in their defence of inevitable accident. In consequence, they did not pay damages to the owners of Storborg because they were not liable against them. Of course, the underwriters of the owners avoided the possibility of paying damages to the assured owners under clause 8 of Institute Time Clauses Hulls (*ITCH*) (*collision liability clause*). Also, next Chapter.

[5] Hill (pp. 258 – 282) analyses the International Regulations for the prevention of collisions at sea. For the application of the Convention by the Hellenic courts see Piraeus Court of First Instance (ΠΠΠΠειρ) 4883 / 2004, Review of Maritime Law (ΕΝΔ) 32 (2004) 438 [collision between a Malta-flag vessel and a Cyprus-flag vessel in Greek territorial navigable waters]. Also see Piraeus Court of Appeal (ΕφΠειρ) 289 / 2005, Review of Maritime Law (ΕΝΔ) 33 (2005) 196. For the international law aspects and the role of the IMO see Balkin and the International Convention on the Inter-governmental Maritime Consultative Organization 1948. Also, see Oral, p. 3 for statistic elements and analysis of collisions between vessels, especially tankers, in the Turkish Straits.

aircraft, helicopter or similar objects[6] or with any external object other than water. In all these cases[7], the insurer shall indemnify the assured for any loss of or damage to the subject – matter insured. For example, in *Mancomunidad*[8] a vessel collided with ice. It was held that ice falls within the meaning of 'any external object' and ice is not water which is an expressly excluded peril under the Institute Cargo Clauses (B) and (C), clause 4.1.4.. In *Reischer*[9] a ship was insured against damage received in collision with any object. She collided with a snag, the cover of her condenser was broken and it had to be abandoned (abandonment in this sense and in the sense of the right of the assured to abandonment is discussed in the next Part). The Court of Appeal held that the loss by the collision was covered. Lindley LJ said: 'it would in my opinion be contrary to *good sense* to hold that the damage by the sinking was not covered by this policy'[10].

In the discussed clauses no reference is made to any insurance cover of possible liability of the assured to third parties (for example, the owners of the harbour equipment). The only liability cover offered by a marine hull policy is liability consequent upon collision between the insured ship and another ship or vessel[11].

However, liability due to the vessel running into a dock wall, breakwater or anything that is not another ship is o f t e n expressly included[12].

Second, in the collision liability clause collision with other vessel means physical contact of the insured vessel with 'a hollow structure intended to do its real work upon the sea, and which is capable of free and ordered movement from one place to another'[13]. This is called the test of navigability[14].

Third, collision with other vessel means (under the collision liability clause) collision with the anchor (part) of another vessel[15], with a tug[16] or with a third

---

[6] ITCH, clauses (*cl*) 6.1.6, 6.2.5; Institute Voyage Clauses Hulls (*IVCH*), cl 4.1.6, 4.2.5; Institute Time Clauses Freight (*ITCF*), cl 7.1.6, 7.2.5; Institute Voyage Clauses Freight (*IVCF*), cl 4.1.6, 4.2.5.

[7] They are subject to the Paramount Clause (cl 24 – 27 of the ITCH) as it is explained in n.1.

[8] (1927) 1 KB 567.

[9] (1894) 2 QB 548.

[10] (1894) 2 QB 548, 551.

[11] Brown, p.18.

[12] Arnould, p.668, n. 86.

[13] *Per* Atkinson J in *Polpen* (1943) 1 All ER 162, 165.

[14] It was first applied in *Chandler* (1898) 1 QB 32.

[15] *Re Margetts* (1901) 2 KB 792.

[16] *McCowan (The Niobe)* (1891) AC 401. While *The Niobe* was being towed, her tug, *Flying Serpent*, came into collision and sank the *Valetta* whose owners recovered damages both from *The Niobe* and the tug. The owners of *The Niobe* sued the hull underwriters for the indemnity under the collision liability clause. The Earl of Selborne, in the House of Lords, said that collision is not only direct contact but also collision between the tug and the vessel insured. 'Damage done by the tug to the *Valetta* was damage done by the tow' *per* Phillimore J in *Re Margetts* (1901) 2 KB 792.

vessel[17] (indirect collision: no actual physical contact). 'Other vessel' does not embrace nets[18], a gas float used as a floating beacon[19], a pontoon crane[20], a flying boat[21] or the wreck of another vessel unless 'the *reasonably minded* owner would continue salvage operations in the hope of completely recovering the vessel by those operations and subsequent repair.'[22] This means that a collision of the insured vessel with the *objects* just described is not covered under the collision liability clause and the underwriter shall not indemnify the assured for his liability to third parties.

Finally, at to whether a vessel falls within the 'other vessel'[23] in the collision liability clause may best be determined by the 'elephant test' suggested by Scrutton LJ in the Court of Appeal in *Merchants*[24]. He said: 'One might possibly take the position of the gentleman who dealt with the elephant by saying that he could not define an elephant, but he knew what it was when he saw one.'

b. Hellenic marine insurance law

Collision with other vessel is a maritime peril[25]. In principle, every maritime peril is covered by the 'all risks' principle[26] which is a traditional[27] feature of Hellenic marine insurance law. If the insurer wishes to exempt a specific maritime peril from the insurance policy, it is his duty to describe it in written and

---

[17] *William France* (1915) 3 KB 290. The facts were as follows. The insured vessel (Cornwoods) collided with Rouen and Rouen collided with Galatée. Did Cornwoods collide with Galatée? Swinfen Eady LJ held that '[there is] a collision between his ship (*Cornwoods*) and another ship (*Galatée*), although the damage is not immediately and directly caused by the actual impact between the two colliding vessels.' (1915) 3 KB 290, 301.

[18] 'Nets are not a part of the ship' (as the anchor is considered to be, n.14) *per* Lord Reading CJ in *Bennett* (1914) 3 KB 61.

[19] This was 'because it was not constructed for the purpose of being navigated or of conveying cargo'. *Gas Float* (1897) AC 337.

[20] *Merchants* (1926) 32 Com Cas 165; 26 LlLRep 201.

[21] 'A seaplane's real work is to fly' in *Polpen* (1943) 1 All ER 162, 165.

[22] *Per* Greer J in *Pelton* (1925) 22 LlLRep 510, KBD.

[23] It is a different issue whether the other vessel is in a warlike operation, is pirate or belongs to the same owner. The latter is discussed in the next Chapter. Public vessels do not fall within the scope of the Brussels Convention (article 11). However, sections 1 and 2 of the Maritime Conventions Act 1911 (*liability shall be in proportion to the degree in which each vessel was in fault*) shall apply in the case of vessels belonging to His Majesty as they apply in the case of other vessels (section 6 of the Crown Proceedings Act 1947).

[24] *Merchants* (1926) 32 Com Cas 165; 26 LlLRep 201.

[25] Article 269 of the Code (ΚΙΝΔ); Doukas, p.151; Rokas I., p.105; Rokas K., p.47; Skantzakis, p.198; Skouloudis, p.383.

[26] 'The 'all risks' principle is subject to the opposite agreement of the insurer and the assured and they may set the (English) institute time clauses'. Athens Court of First Instance (ΠΠΑθ) 3831 /1979, 10 ΕΝΔ 30. Athens Court of Appeal (ΕφΑθ) 6191 /1981, 33 ΕΕΔ 263. In all cases, if the collision is a covered peril, it is subject to war risks (article 272(1) of the Code (ΚΙΝΔ)). This reminds us the English *paramount clause*.

[27] Argyriadis, p.111. The English law follows the opposite principle of the 'specified perils'.

clear terms; otherwise, it is deemed by law that the underwriter shall cover every maritime peril. This principle operates in favour of the shipowner. Even if the master or the crew has been negligent, the insurer is still legally[28] bound to cover the loss of or damage to the subject – matter insured.

In case of a collision which was an inevitable accident, article 235 of the Hellenic Code of Private Maritime Law (Code (KINΔ)) provides that the damages shall be borne by those who have suffered them. This is the adoption of the second article of the Brussels Conventions. As we have already seen, this rule stands also in the United Kingdom. If one or both vessels are to blame, then there is a statutory provision (article 269) of the Code (KINΔ). In its first paragraph the 'all risks' principle is settled. The second paragraph reads: 'The insurer is liable for all damages the ship, because of collision, is obliged to pay to third parties, except damages relating to harm to the body or the health.' This means that the collision liability (of the owner of the vessel) is, in principle and by law, a covered peril.

As for the issues dealt with in the previous paragraph we present here the meaning of collision with other vessel.

First, collision is the violent physical contact of the insured vessel with other vessel or vessels. The indirect collision is not a collision in the legal and technical sense of the term but it is regulated by analogy by law[29] as if it were a collision. In simple terms, indirect collision is a collision covered (as it is in the United Kingdom) but the reasoning for this cover is different. In addition, the legal term for contact with any external object is 'striking' instead of 'collision'. It is a covered peril (because of the 'all risks' principle) but the liability of the assured against third parties in respect thereof is not covered unless the policy states something else[30].

Second, collision with other vessel means violent physical contact of a vessel with 'every vessel[31] of whatsoever tonnage and every navigable ship moving at the sea, lake, navigable waters or in the air above them[32], capable or not capable of independent movement'[33] as article 1(2) of the Law Decree 551 / 1970 provides for the meaning of 'vessel' in marine insurance.

---

[28] Article 274 of the Code (KINΔ).

[29] This is the law regulating the international settlement of the damages between the colliding vessels. Papapolitis, p. 185.

[30] Article 1(1)c of the Law Decree 551 /1970 (as amended by the Presidential Decree 118 /1985) provides that any liability against third parties may be covered under a marine insurance policy. The collision liability is specifically regulated (article 269 (2) of the Code (KINΔ)).

[31] 'Every vessel' is broader than 'hollow structure'.

[32] This means that a flying boat is 'other vessel'.

[33] On the contrary, in United Kingdom law 'the vessel must be capable of free and ordered movement'. Furthermore, there is no Hellenic requirement of the English '*real work upon the sea*' (n. 12).

Third, collision with other vessel[34] means collision with the anchor of the other vessel or between vessels at anchors[35], with a flying boat[36], a pontoon crane[37], a gas float used as a floating beacon[38].

'Other vessel' does not embrace nets[39] or wrecks (in any condition)[40]. In Hellenic law, the judgments of the courts are often different as the courts are permitted to interpret the same provisions in any chosen way, even if such interpretation runs against a previous judgment of another or the same court. Only if the judgments are the same for a very long period, they might create law. But even then, it is possible that a court may decide differently. In the context of the discussed topic the courts[41] have taken the view of a narrower definition of 'other vessel' by applying the criterion of '*capable of independent movement*'. However, the later judgements[42] (followed those applying that criterion) seem to accept the broader definition of a vessel (*capable or not capable of independent movement*) even before the adoption of article 1(2) of the Law Decree 551 / 1970.

Finally, the statutory definition of a vessel in Hellenic marine insurance differs from the statutory definition of a vessel in Hellenic private maritime law (article 1(1) of the Code (ΚΙΝΔ) requires the element of 'capable of independent movement')[43]. Whether a particular object is or is not a vessel is a question of

---

[34] A trailer, second wagon of a lorry, collided with another lorry. It was held that the trailer is 'another vehicle' within the meaning of motor vehicle insurance law. Athens Court of Appeal (ΕφΑθ) 3245 /1985, 13 (ΙΓ΄) (1985) ΕπΣυγκΔ 400. This is a similarity to Hellenic marine insurance. The contrary applies in other cases, like it is explained in n.34.

[35] Report of the Committee on Title Twelve of the Code (ΚΙΝΔ). Also, in motor vehicle collision insurance the opposite rule applies. A moving vehicle collided with another vehicle which was parked and that non moving vehicle was held not to be 'another vehicle'. Athens Court of Appeal (ΕφΑθ) 2234 /1974, 2 (Β΄) (1974) ΕπΣυγκΔ 254; Thessaloniki Court of Appeal (ΕφΘεσ) 156 /1979, (1980) Αρμ 565; Corinth Court of First Instance (ΠΠΚορ) 306 /1969, (1969) Αρμ 778.

[36] This has been already clarified in n.31.

[37] Areios Pagos (ΑΠ) 347 /1938, 50 (Ν΄) Θ 161; Piraeus Court of First Instance (ΠΠΠειρ) 774 /1928, 6 (ΣΤ΄) Δικ 126. Also, Papamichalopoulos, p.16; Spiliopoulos, p.140.

[38] It is capable of being moved, therefore, it is a vessel.

[39] Argyriadis (p. 114), Doukas (p. 151) and Papapolitis (p. 182) state that nets are not part of the vessel in the meaning of (1)1a of the Law Decree 551 /1970, unless there is an opposite agreement.

[40] Athens Court of Appeal (ΕφΑθ) 1760 /1981, 22 ΕλλΔικ 637. Also, Achis, p. 240; Kiantos, p.105.

[41] Council of State (ΣτΕ) 63 /1953, 4 (Δ΄) ΕΕΔ 65; Athens Court of Appeal (ΕφΑθ) 1444 /1954, 65 (ΞΕ΄) Θ 1026. A vessel is thereby defined as 'capable of independent movement'. Karavas (p. 33) refers to judgments which have taken the opposite view.

[42] As it is said in n. 40.

[43] 'Ship, for the purposes of this Code, is every vessel of 10 tonnage intended to move independently upon the sea'. As it has been said, this definition does not apply to marine insurance where 'every navigable ship' is a vessel (article 1(2) of the Code (ΚΙΝΔ)). Article 1 of the Law Decree 551 /1970 was introduced in Hellenic marine insurance in 1970, namely 12

fact[44]. Nevertheless, the definition of article 1(2) of the Law Decree is always the starting point for the Hellenic courts in collision marine insurance cases. This is because of the *lex specialis* rule. Also, article 1(2) of the Code states that the article 1(1) definition shall not apply to Title Twelve (collision between vessels, articles 235 – 245) and Title Fourteen (marine insurance, articles 257 – 288) of the Code (ΚΙΝΔ).

c. Comparison

Collision is considered as an (insurable) peril of the sea. In English law, the courts (*The Xantho*) settled the rule. In Hellenic law, the Parliament introduced the rule by the legislation of the Code (ΚΙΝΔ) in the Title Fourteen (marine insurance).

The common law and the civil law arrived to the same result, even if their legal nature differs. For example, the same content of the English paramount c l a u s e is found in article 272(1) of the Code (ΚΙΝΔ).

A far more important difference relates to the fact that English marine insurance law recognises the 'enumerated risks' principle[45]. Collision and collision liability is covered only if this is specified in the marine insurance policy. On the contrary, such perils are covered automatically under the Hellenic provisions (article 269 of the Code (ΚΙΝΔ). This is the traditional 'all risks' principle. Only if there is a specific exclusion clause[46], is collision and collision liability not covered in Hellenic law. This shows that the shipowner is more protected in this legal order. However, in practice this legal difference may not mean much. In practice, most Hellenic owners of the vessels assure them in London for a number of reasons[47].

Collision with other vessel in the Hellenic law receives a broader scope than in United Kingdom law[48]. This is because the Law Decree 551 / 1970 governing marine insurance in parallel to Title Fourteen of the Code (ΚΙΝΔ) introduces a wider definition of vessel than the English common law and statutory definition.

---

years after the Code had been in legal existence (1958). In the United Kingdom, section 742 of the Merchant Shipping Acts (1894) (1898) (1921) provides for 'every ship or boat or every other vessel used in navigation'.

[44] Hodges (p. 317) refers to *Gas Float* in the context of United Kingdom law. In Hellenic law this is widely accepted by the authors as the courts may interpret the law in different (even contradictory) ways.

[45] Wight, Lecture 5 /3 /1999, School of Law, Essex.

[46] Any exclusion is subject to article 281 of the Hellenic Civil Code (AK) which prohibits abuse of rights in the context of civil law (in consequence, in the context of marine insurance law as it is part of the Code of P r i v a t e Maritime law).

[47] Papapolitis, p.122.

[48] Nevertheless, wrecks are not 'other vessels' whatsoever the case may be. In the motor vehicle insurance, vehicle is narrowly defined. Areios Pagos (ΑΠ) 146 /1973, 21 NoB 899. Thessaloniki Court of First Instance (ΠΠΘεσ) 2177 /1978, 8 (Η΄) (1980) ΕπΣυγκΔ 342. Also, *supra*.

In a metaphorical expression we would say that the Hellenic law expands the definition of other vessel up to the air (flying boats, article 1 of Law Decree 551 / 1970) whilst the English law extends it down to the *corpus* of the sea (wrecks subject to the test *per* Greer J in *Pelton*[49]). Of course, the wide scope of the Hellenic definition of 'other vessel'[50] operates in favour of the assured of the subject – matter insured. On the other hand, United Kingdom law appears to be preferable to the Hellenic one for the underwriters. They are liable in fewer cases under the former law than in the latter.

There are similarities between the two legal orders. In principle, no liability is covered by the policies for damages paid by the assured to third parties upon collision of the vessel insured with an object (dock walls or any proprietary object[51]). Or, a collision of the insured vessel with an anchor (part) of other vessel is collision with other vessel. There are, however, differences stemming from the different *philosophy* of the two legal systems. In the Hellenic Republic[52], 'striking' differs from 'collision'. In the United Kingdom, Mathew J said: 'I cannot distinguish collision with from striking against'[53]). The Hellenic definition of 'collision' is a 'violent physical contact'. In consequence, the insurer covers damages to third vessel caused by the collision of the insured vessel with other vessel only by analogy by law. In the United Kingdom, Walton J said: 'The precise nature of the 'contact' is a matter of some difficulty'[54]. The following incident highlights what we describe as different philosophy. In 1909, the British Delegation suggested that the Brussels Convention should apply to collision of vessels with objects other than vessels. The Hellenic Delegation rejected (along with the other ones) that suggestion[55].

---

[49] (1925) 22 LlLRep 510, KBD

[50] For example, 'hollow structure' is not required in Hellenic marine insurance law in relation to the definition 'other vessel' in collision cases.

[51] An iceberg is not *prima facie* such object.

[52] Hellas or Greece. For the application of the UK Marine Insurance Act 1906 from the Hellenic courts see Areios Pagos (ΑΠ) 1651 / 2005, Review of Maritime Law (ΕΝΔ) 33 (2005), 241, Piraeus Court of Appeal (ΕφΠειρ) 773 / 2005, Review of Maritime Law (ΕΝΔ) 34 (2006), 20, Piraeus Court of Appeal (ΕφΠειρ) 704 / 2005, Review of Maritime Law (ΕΝΔ) 33 (2005), 247, Piraeus Court of Appeal (ΕφΠειρ) 62 / 2005, Review of Maritime Law (ΕΝΔ) 33 (2005), 256, Piraeus Court of Appeal (ΕφΠειρ) 1141 / 2004, Review of Maritime Law (ΕΝΔ) 32 (2004), 440, Piraeus One Member Court of First Instance (ΜΠΠειρ) 5794 / 2005, Review of Maritime Law (ΕΝΔ) 34 (2006), 30.

[53] *Union* (1895) 2 QB 279, 281. In *Hough* Grove J said: 'Collision … may be that one (vessel) is active and the other is passive, but still, in one sense, they each strike the other'. (1885) 861, 864.

[54] *Costain* (The Nassau Bay) (1979) 1 Lloyd's Rep 395, 406.

[55] Proceedings of Session 18 September to 8 October 1909, pp. 70 – 71.

C. Collision liability

a. United Kingdom marine insurance law

Collision liability is the subject – matter insured under the collision liability clause. The owner of the vessel insured will probably be liable in the future against third parties if his insured vessel collides with other vessel. In collisions caused by *force majeure*, proved to be inevitable accident or the causes of which have remained in doubt, there is no liability of any vessel or owner of the colliding vessels. Article 2 of Brussels Convention reads: 'damages shall be borne by those who have suffered them'. In other words, there is no subject – matter against which the owner may be assured.

On the contrary, if one vessel is to blame, then the owner of the insured vessel becomes legally liable to third parties, *inter alia*, for any loss of or damage to the other vessel and property thereon. This liability practically means that he has to pay certain amounts of money to third parties. If he wishes to recover them, he may assure his respective liability. The fact is that it is not certain that he may be liable for the collision. This uncertainty relating to the peril is necessary in marine insurance for any one who wishes to become part of a policy. Insurance against a certain event (for example, the owner states: *I will cause a collision of my vessel with a huge iceberg with the intention to cause its sinking*) does not exist[56].

The analysis of the collision liability clause consists of the three – fourths liability of the underwriters' doctrine, the upper limit to the liability of the underwriters and its prerequisites. Also, in this Chapter we deal with the scope of the recoverable damages, the excluded damages that the assured pay to third parties and cannot recover and the single liability principle which governs in the first place the calculation of the damages that each party shall pay to the other.

aa. Three – fourths underwriter's collision liability

Clause 8.1 of the Institute Time Clauses Hulls (95) provides that 'the Underwriters agree to indemnify the Assured for three – fourths of *any sum or sums paid* by the Assured to any other person or persons by reason of the Assured becoming legally liable by way of damages ... where such payment by the Assured is in consequence of the Vessel hereby insured coming into collision with any other vessel'.

The rule of the clause is that the insurer is not liable to cover the full amount of the damages paid by the assured to third parties in respect of collision, but the insurer is liable only for the three – fourths of the damages paid by the assured. Three – fourths is the *quota* of the damages paid by the assured. It is a way of calculation the indemnity that the insurer must pay to the assured. In theory, the reason for this settlement is that the assured is encouraged to exercise due care and attention. In practice, this is not the case. The assured does not run the re-

[56] Wight, Lecture 5 /3 /1999, School of Law, Essex.

maining one – fourth of the risks[57]. This one – fourth is absorbed by the Protection and Indemnity Associations (P & I Associations or Clubs)[58].

In 1868 it was held in *Xenos*[59] that c o s t s incurred by the assured in successfully defending an action brought by the owners of another colliding vessel were n o t recoverable as 'damages' paid to third parties in respect of collision. Today, the law has changed. Clause 8.3 of the ITCH (95) provides that 'the Underwriters will also pay three – fourths of the legal costs incurred by the Assured or which the Assured may be compelled to pay in contesting liability or taking proceedings to limit liability, with the prior written consent of the Underwriters'. L e g a l costs does not just mean l a w y e r s' costs. It will include disbursements, such as witness and experts f e e s which are incurred for the preparation and presentation of the case of the assured[60].

There is an issue relating to 'costs of attack and costs of defence' which we do not purport to discuss in the present text[61]. As far as limitation of liability concerns, we briefly mention that this is a right of the assured shipowner[62]. For example, in a collision claim he may limit his liability against third parties according to the value of his ship. This seems to be fair. Denning LJ[63] has stated that such limitation of liability 'is *not* a matter of justice, it is a rule of public policy'.

O'May mentions that the discussed limitation of liability has an effect on the apportionment of damages. For instance, in a both to blame collision, where each vessel should pay one half of the other's ship damages, such equalization is distorted if one of the vessels limits by law the damages payable by her. The impact of limitation of liability in the context of marine insurance has to be taken into account in calculating the measure of indemnity under the collision liability clause[64].

---

[57] Hodges, p.318. Kalantzis, p.50.

[58] The owners of the vessels have founded Mutual Insurance Associations or Clubs which cover, *inter alia*, protection and indemnity, especially liability against third party. Bennett, p.236. Papapolitis, pp. 274, 280.

[59] (1868) LR 3; CP 630; 17 WR 893.

[60] O'May, p. 237.

[61] Goodacre (pp. 409 – 414) and Hodges (pp. 319 – 320) deals with the matter and states that 'an assured who has failed in his defence is entitled to recover from the underwriters three – fourths of the total legal costs for defending the suit'. Hodges (p. 320) also points out that in practice, however, no distinction is likely to drawn between costs of attack and costs of defence; costs is generally awarded as a single sum.

[62] In United Kingdom law the statutory right of the owner of the vessel to limit his liability stems from the Merchant Shipping Acts 1979 (based on the Convention on Limitation of Liability in Maritime Claims 1976).

[63] The Bramley Moore (1963) 2 Lloyd's Rep 429.

[64] O'May, p.212.

bb. Upper limit to the liability of the underwriter

Clause 8.2.2 of the collision liability clause (ITCH (95)) provides: 'in no case shall the Underwriters' total liability under Clauses 8.1 and 8.2 exceed their proportionate part of three – fourths of the insured value of the Vessel hereby insured in respect of any one collision'.

Clause 8.2 states that 'this indemnity provided by this clause 8 shall be *in addition to* the indemnity provided by the other terms and conditions of this insurance...'

All in all, the insurer could be made liable in respect of up to 175% of the insured value of the vessel insured[65]. To this, an additional sum of three – quarters of the legal costs incurred by the assured has to be added.

Additional insurance on Excess or Increased Value of Hull and Machinery for a sum not exceeding 25 per cent of the value stated[66] is permitted[67]. The amount payable is the proportion of the difference of the three – fours of collision liability, which is not recoverable under the hull and machinery insurance because of the limit therein based on the insured value, as the amount insured bears to the total sum insured against excess liability[68].

cc. Scope of the damages recoverable. The Sistership Clause.

The collision liability clause covers only collision damages payable in respect of a tort[69]. In consequence, it does n o t cover collision damages to vessels if the colliding vessels belong to the same owner. Indeed, no liability in tort arises, as a person cannot bring an action against himself[70].

Nevertheless, there is one other clause for colliding *sisterships* (vessels belong to the same owner). Clause 9 of the ITCH (95) provides that 'the liability for the collision or the amount payable for the services rendered shall be referred to a sole arbitrator ... to be agreed between the Underwriters and the Assured'.

---

65 The insurer could be liable for the full extent (of the insured value) for the damage sustained by the insured vessel and up to three – quarters of the insured value in relation to third party liability. Hodges, pp. 320 – 321.

66 'A valued policy is a policy which specifies the agreed value of the subject – matter insured', section 27(2) of the Act. Section 28 of the Act states that 'an unvalued policy is a policy which does not specify the value of the subject – matter insured, but, subject to the limit of the sum insured, leaves the insurable value to be subsequently ascertained, in the manner herein – before specified'.

67 The Disbursements Warranty Clause of the ITCH (83), 21.1.1.

68 O'May, p. 245.

69 This is discussed in the next paragraph.

70 Ivamy, p. 174. Martin (p.467) states that tort originates in the Latin *tortus* and tort in old French (harm).

If this were not so[71], Underwriters would simply pay for the damage suffered by each vessel and the ship-owner would not recover any part of his *demurrage*[72].

The damages for which an indemnity is given under the collision liability clause in consequence of a collision are for:
(8.1.1) loss of or damage to any other vessel or property on any other vessel;
(8.1.2) delay to or loss of use of any such other vessel or property thereon;
(8.1.3) general average of, salvage of, or salvage under contract of, any such other vessel or property thereon.

Under cl 8.1.1 the indemnity only relates to physical loss or damage to the other vessel or property on board it. 'Property' is very wide and includes cargo on board, containers[73], gear and appurtenances.

In the light of cl 8.1.2 we must distinguish between delay to the insured vessel and delay to the other vessel. Damages due to detention of the insured vessel during repairs necessitated by a collision are not recoverable under the policy on the insured vessel as damages due to collision, under either the collision liability clause or the cover in the hull policy. On the other hand, damages for delay to a colliding vessel or property on that vessel are covered under the collision liability clause[74]. Delay or loss of use of a third vessel (as in *William France*[75]) would also come within the respective coverage.

Finally, collisions may give rise to general average sacrifice and to a need for salvage assistance. In *Owners*[76] it was held that cargo's contribution to gen-

---

[71] Goodacre, p.429.

[72] This means damages payable under a charterparty at a specified daily rate for any (demurrage) days required for completing the loading or discharging the cargo after the lay days have expired. Lay days are the number of days specified in a charterparty to enable the charterer (shipowner) to load or discharge cargo. Martin, pp.135, 260. Brown (p. 208) states that the expression commonly used in marine insurance to define loss of use consequent upon collision is 'demurrage', although, in fact, the term 'demurrage' really means damages payable under a charterparty (like it is stated in this note).

[73] On the 24th of August 1999 cargo vessel *Ever Decent* from Taiwan collided with the cruise vessel *Norwegian Dream* from Norway, in the English Channel (30 nautical miles away from the port of Margate). *Ever Decent* was carrying 15 containers (most of which were full of liquid paints). In consequence of the collision, 24 passengers of the Norwegian ship were injured and part of the cargo was destroyed. TO BHMA (To Vima, The Step), 25 /8 /1999, p. A8 (International News).
Three – fourths of the damages (possibly) paid by the owner of *Norwegian Dream* (provided that he was liable) in respect of the destroyed containers would be recovered by him from the insurers under the English collision liability clause.
On the contrary, damages (possibly) paid by the owner of *Ever Decent* (provided that he was liable) in respect of the personal injuries of the 24 passengers would not be recovered. The exclusions of the liability of the underwriters in such case is discussed in paragraph ff.

[74] O'May, p. 233.

[75] (1915) 3 KB 290, CA.

[76] (1947) AC 265; 80 LlLRep 55, HL. Section 66(2) of the Act defines 'general average' as an 'extraordinary sacrifice or expenditure voluntarily and reasonably made or incurred in time of peril'.

eral average resulting from the collision of the two vessels was recoverable in damages from the colliding vessel to the extent that that vessel was to blame for the collision. 'Salvage charges' are the charges recoverable under maritime law by a salvor independently of contract[77]. Expenses paid by the assured in order to save the vessel or cargo insured are not covered[78] under the collision liability clause.

dd. Prerequisites for the application of the collision liability clause

(i) *Any sum or sums paid by the Assured*

Clause 8.1 provides that 'the Underwriters agree to indemnify the Assured for three – fourths of any sum or sums paid by the Assured ...'. The principle that the assured can only recover part of what he has paid to third parties (because of his collision liability) is highlighted in *Thompson*[79]. The assured's vessel was sold by order of the Admiralty Court and the proceeds paid to the owner of the colliding vessel in satisfaction of the damages awarded in collision proceedings. Although the sale was for less than her full market value, the amount recoverable under the collision liability clause was no more than three – fourths of the proceeds of the forced sale. In practice, proof of payment is required[80] before the assured could be indemnified for liability to third parties upon collision.

Two legal aspects arising in the discussed context are the following. First, it has yet to be decided[81] whether actual payment is a condition precedent to entitlement to indemnification or merely serves to reinforce the limitation of cover to the extent of exposure to third party liability. Hodges[82] uses the term 'prerequisite'. Also, as regards legal costs payment is not a condition precedent[83].

Second, payment by the assured can also be important having regard to the rights conferred upon third parties by the Third Parties (Rights against Insurers) Act 1930 (*the Act 1930*). Section 1(1) of the Act 1930 provides that if the assured against liability to third parties (for instance, collision liability clause in a policy) becomes bankrupt (winding – up for companies insured), the rights of the insured shall be transferred to and vest in the third party to whom the liability was so incurred. Section 1(3) of the Act 1930 provides that a contract of in-

---

[77] Section 65(2) of the Act. In *The Vandyck* (1887) 7 PD 42, 46, Sir Phillimore awarded salvage against two ships which were disentangled by salvors following a collision.

[78] Grime (p.248) refers to expenses arising from the duty of the assured to take measures under section 78(4) of the Act.

[79] (1857) 26 LJQB 93.

[80] Arnould, p. 665; Hodges, p. 322; O'May, p. 222.

[81] Bennett, p. 175.

[82] P. 322.

[83] Arnould, p.665, n. 80; O'May, p. 222. A condition precedent is a provision that does not form part of the contractual obligation but operates to suspend the contract until a specified event has happened. Martin, p. 94. Also, Beale, p. 485; McKendrick, p. 180.

surance shall be of no effect, if it purports to alter the rights of the parties. Section 1 (4) of the Act 1930 states: 'upon a transfer under subsection (1) of this section, the insurer shall, subject to section three of this Act (settlement between insurers and insured persons) be under the same liability to the third party as he would have been under to the insured'.

The question which arises in relevance to the Act 1930 is whether the payment of the damages by the assured is a condition precedent to liability of underwriters. If the answer is affirmative, then the third party would be deprived of any rights under the policy because of section 1(4) of the Act 1930. In 1935 the answer was affirmative[84].

In 1990 the House of Lords also gave an affirmative answer in *The Fanti* and *The Padre Island* which were heard together.

A 'pay to be paid' provision in the P & I Club rules sets the *condition precedent* that before the insured could be paid by tbe association, he has first to prove that he had paid the third party (discharged his liability). Staughton J (in *The Fanti*) held that that provision in the P & I Club rules was rendered nugatory[85] by section 1(3) of the Act 1930. On the contrary, Lord Brandon of Oakbrook found[86] that Saville J (in *The Padre Island*) was right as Saville J held[87] (*as opposed to Staughton J*) that the 'pay to be paid' provision was not rendered nugatory by section 1(3) of the Act 1930. In consequence, the law is that no rights are transferred to a third party under the Act 1930 in the event that the assured shipowner is wound up without payment of the collision liability or part of it.

(ii) *Legally liable*

As we have seen, the collision liability clause does not apply if the collision resulted from *force majeure*[88], or its causes were in doubt, or it was an inevitable accident[89]. The assured must be legally liable to third parties in respect of colli-

[84] In *Re Nautilus* (1935) 52 LlLRep 183, 189, Maugham LJ said: 'under the present policy the liability in strictness applies o n l y if the assured becomes liable not only to pay but shall pay ... actual sums in question'. In that case it was also held that the Act 1930 applies to claims under the collision liability clause.

[85] (1989) 1 Lloyd's Rep 239.

[86] (1990) 2 Lloyd's Rep 191, 197, HL.

[87] (1984) 1 Lloyd's Rep 408.

[88] In French it means irresistible compulsion or coercion. The phrase is used particularly in commercial contracts to describe events possibly affecting the contract and that are completely outside the parties' control (acts of God, *storms, floods, earthquakes*) Martin, p.193. On the 27th of July 1999 a cargo vessel collided with another cargo vessel in the Northeast Aegean Sea (between Tenedos and Limnos Islands). On the television they said that the fog in that area at the time of the collision was extremely terrible. No one could see anything. This may be classified as a collision due to *force majeure*.

[89] It means an accident that could not have been prevented by the exercise of ordinary care and skill. Martin, p. 232. It seems that the clear distinction between *force majeure* and inevitable accident is not always an easy test. We could say that an inevitable accident could have

sion, if he wishes to recover any sum paid by him, provided that the other prerequisites of the collision liability clause are fulfilled.

(iii) *By way of damages*

The collision liability clause covers only collision damages payable in respect of a tort. It does not cover liability arising in contract. In *Furness*[90] a vessel being assisted by an Admiralty tug was in collision with the tug due to negligent navigation of the tug. Under the towage contract the shipowners agreed 'to make good to the Admiralty all damage'. The assured owner of the vessel paid the amount of the damage to the Admiralty, and claimed an indemnity from the insurer under the collision liability clause. Branson J said[91]: 'The expression 'by way of damages' indicates liability arising by way of tort and not by way of contract. There is no such liability here'.

(iv) *In consequence of collision*

The collision liability clause covers only damages paid in consequence of collision. This means that the principle of causation also applies under the wording 'in consequence of'[92]. Only if the liability of the assured proximately caused by the collision does the collision liability clause come into force.

In *Hall*[93] a vessel arrived off Dunkirk and a pilot boat belonging to the French Pilotage Administration collided with the vessel and damaged herself. The pilot boat's steering was defective. The insured vessel was in no way to blame. However, under the French pilotage law, the shipowners were obliged to pay for the repairs to the French pilot boat.

The Court of Appeal held that the shipowners had had to pay for the repairs of the pilot boat, 'not in consequence of the collision, but in consequence of French law'[94]. The payment was not a liability proximately caused by the collision. Therefore, the payment was not recoverable from the underwriters under the collision liability clause as section 55(1) of the Act states that 'the insurer ... is not liable for any loss which is not proximately caused by a peril insured against'[95].

---

been prevented by the exercise of e x t r a – ordinary care and skill, whereas *force majeure* may cause a collision irrespective of any human care and skill exercised for the prevention of the casualty.

[90] (1936) 55 LlLRep 52; 2 KB 461; 2 All ER 119, KBD.

[91] (1936) 2 All ER 119, 120, KBD.

[92] Goodacre, p.408.

[93] (1939) 1 KB 748; 1 All ER 809, CA.

[94] This case may be seen from another angle. For instance, Hodges (p. 321) states that 'by way of damages' does not extent to damages which arise as a matter of a statutory right to indemnity. Hodges ends up saying that the payment was made in consequence of the application of French law. This may fall within the prerequisite 'in consequence of' under the collision liability clause.

[95] As we have already said, it is impossible to deal with the legal aspects regarding proximate causation in the present text (for example, what constitutes proximate cause, whether the last

ee. Single liability

Clause 8.2.1 of the collision liability clause provides that 'where the insured Vessel is in collision with another vessel and both vessels are to blame then, unless the liability of one or both vessels becomes limited by law, the indemnity under this Clause 8 shall be calculated on the principle of cross – liabilities'[96].

Cross – liabilities is a legal principle on which the indemnity is calculated under clause 8.2.1 if both colliding vessels are to blame. Even in such case the calculation of the indemnity is based on the principle of single liability, if the liability of one or both vessels becomes limited by law[97]. In Admiralty law, the principal rule is calculation of indemnity on single liability[98]. If one vessel is to blame, there is no need for calculation as the innocent third party receives damages from the other shipowner. But if both vessels are to blame (equally, or in different degrees), then the necessary calculation of the damages is based on the single liability principle. This means the following.

Whoever owner has suffered the lesser of the damage shall have to pay. There is (for the purposes of law) one liability. Therefore, there is one payment. This principle in English common law has been established in *The Khedive*[99] since 1882 when this principle has also been introduced in United States law in *The North Star*[100]. As for the degree of fault, it is settled that the damage is apportioned equally if different degrees of fault cannot be established (unlike the old Admiralty rule under which the damage was apportioned equally in any case)[101]. Under the Maritime Conventions Act 1911 the liability to make good the damage or loss is in proportion to the degree in which each vessel was at fault.

Single liability was the method of calculation of damages in marine insurance as it was held in *The Balnacraig*[102]. In that case it was held that having received a payment of the balance due from the other vessel, *the Balnacraig* was unable to recover under the running down clause (the collision liability clause at that time). The assured vessel (*the Balnacraig*) was unable to recover any part of the

---

cause in the time chain of events is the proximate cause, and so forth). (Bennett, pp. 115 – 135). In the context of the discussed issues, we may give an example of a cause which was held to have been *too remote* which best illustrates what is not a proximate cause. Goodacre (p. 409) refers to the *Canadian Transport* which collided with the *Christel Vinnen* in the River Parana resulting in the latter vessel being sunk with her cargo of logs. The vessel was salved but the cargo was detained for a very long time (dispute over payment of salvage), although the logs did not suffer any damage. As a result the cargo owners, who needed the logs to maintain production at their dye works, chartered another vessel to deliver a replacement cargo. It was held that they were not entitled to be reimbursed for the freight paid on the logs brought in replacement, the cost being too remote from the consequence of the collision.

[96] 'As if the respective Owners had been compelled to pay to each other such proportion of each other's damages as may have been properly allowed in ascertaining the balance or sum payable by or to the Assured in consequence of the collision'.

[97] Limitation of liability in the context of marine insurance has already been discussed.

[98] Bennett, p.176.

amount deducted by the other vessel for the damage done to her. The reason was that the insured vessel had not made payment to the other vessels owner.

The principle of cross – liabilities was originally inserted in the body of the collision liability clause to remedy the obviously inequitable position in *the Balnacraig*.

However, cross – liabilities seems to be a preferable method of calculation of indemnity for the underwriters. The figures presented in the books by Arnould[103], Hodges[104] and O'May[105] show that the underwriters pay less the indemnity being calculated on the principle of cross – liabilities than they would have paid if single liability applied. The shipowner who suffered the lesser of the damage has to bear a loss of a higher amount of money in case of application of the cross – liabilities principle. In practice, the Protection and Indemnity (*P & I*) Associations pay more money to that shipowner (who suffered the lesser of the damage) than they would pay if single liability applied.

Cross – liabilities rule in marine insurance was applied to alter the inequitable legal position of the assured, and it seems to operate in favour of the underwriters in comparison to the single liability rule.

ff. Exclusions under clause 8.4 of the collision liability clause [106]

(i) *Removal or disposal of ... thing (cl 8.4.1)*

In addition to the cost of repairs and detention, the owner of a colliding vessel which has been sunk in consequence of collision may, *inter alia*, be able to recover his wreck removal expenses from the owner of the other vessel[107]. Such expenses may arise under statutory powers vested in dock, harbour or other authorities, authorising such authorities to compel the owner of a vessel to light, buoy and remove his vessel, albeit she was not at fault for the collision[108]. Such expenses are not covered under the collision liability clause.

---

[99] (1882) 7 App Cas 795.
[100] (1882) 106 US 17.
[101] Arnould, p.666.
[102] (1889) 24 QBD 663.
[103] P. 666.
[104] Pp. 327 – 328.
[105] Pp. 241 – 242.
[106] Clause 8.4 of the collision liability clause provides: 'Provided always that this Clause 8 shall in no case extend to any sum which the Assured shall pay for …' (and the specific exclusions follow).
[107] The exclusion operates equally whether the sum is paid directly or indirectly to the person who removes or disposes. Bennett, p. 177, n. 34.
[108] O'May, pp. 237 – 238.

(ii) *Real ...property except ...property on other vessels (cl 8.4.2)*

The assured is indemnified only against damages relating solely to other vessels or property on other vessels. The policy under the collision liability clause does not cover real or personal property on the insured vessel.

(iii) *Cargo or other property ...on the insured vessel (cl 8.4.3)*

The conditions of carriage normally exempt the carrier from any liability for damage to cargo arising from collisions[109]. However, it is possible that a contract[110] for the carriage of goods by sea makes the carrier responsible for loss of or damage to cargo in collision casualties. The carrier or shipowner cannot recover any sums paid to the cargo owner under the 8.4.3 exclusion clause.

(iv) *Loss of life, personal injury or illness (cl 8.4.4)*

Liability for loss of life and personal injury is generally covered by P & I Clubs. The liability of the owners of the colliding vessels is joint and several (if both vessels are to blame) and life claimant may recover in full from either vessel. Hull underwriters under cl 8.4.4 are not liable to indemnify the shipowner if he becomes liable against (and has actually paid damages to) life claimants[111]. This is a great difference in marine and motor vehicle insurance in the context of collision claims. The owner of the vehicle (who is usually the driver) must be insured against liability to pay damages for death or bodily injury caused by or arising out of the use of the vehicle[112] (for instance, collision between vehicles). Such cover is compulsory and the insurer is also liable to pay the damages d i r e c t l y to the life claimant (or the third injured party) irrespective of the financial status of the insured[113].

(v) *Pollution or contamination of any real or personal property ... (cl 8.4.5)*

As a consequence of collision at sea, oil or other pollutants may escape or be discharged from a ship and civil or criminal liability may arise. The United Kingdom is a signatory to both the International Convention on Civil Liability for Oil Pollution Damage (1969) and the International Convention on the Estab-

---

109 Goodacre, p. 164. Bennett (p. 177) explains the anomaly in cargo insurance in United States law.

110 The claim of the cargo owner against the carrier might be framed *in tort* (Carver, p. 1451), if the owner of the other vessel was solely responsible for the collision (Wilson, p. 253).

111 Personal injury claims arose after the collision on the 24th of August 1999 between *Ever Decent* and *Norwegian Dream* (n. 72). Also, in consequence of the collision on the 27th of July 1999 between two cargo vessels (n. 87), a member of the crew (third engineer) died. This gave rise to life claim which in the United Kingdom is governed by the Fatal Accidents Act 1976 (Hill, p. 288). For a reported case of collision causing loss of lives see Athens News Agency, *Collision.*

112 Sections 143, 145 of the Road Traffic Act 1988.

113 Section 149 of the Road Traffic Act 1988. Birds (p. 365) and Colinvaux (pp. 421, 454) deal with these legal aspects of motor vehicle insurance.

lishment of an International Fund for Compensation for Oil Pollution Damage (1971)[114].

The Pollution Hazard Clause (clause 7 of the ITCH (95)) allows an assured to recover for any loss of or damage to the insured vessel caused by '*any governmental authority* to prevent a pollution hazard or damage to the environment'. Clause 8.4.5 excludes recovery for any sum which the assured may pay in a collision case for or in respect of pollution or contamination or damage to the environment. This exclusion does not apply to sums payable for salvage remuneration where salvors have worked to prevent damage to the environment. This qualification has been inserted to tie with cl. 10.6 on general average and salvage (ITCH (95)) under which it is specifically declared that such an enhanced salvage award made under article 13(1)b of the International Convention on Salvage (1989) is not excluded from recovery as general average or salvage[115].

b. Hellenic marine insurance law

aa. Four – fourths underwriter's collision liability

Article 269(2) of the Code (KINΔ) provides as follows: 'the insurer is liable for all damages that the ship, because of a collision, is obliged to pay to third parties, except damages relating to harm to the body or health'[116].

The underwriter is liable for the full amount of the sum paid[117] by the assured to third parties after a collision between vessels. It is submitted that the underwriter is also liable to cover the full amount of the legal costs paid by the owner of the vessel to defend himself. The justified reason that the insurer covers such expenses is that the insurer is benefited if either the other vessel has been decided to be at fault or the amount of payable damages has been decided to be lower than the third parties demanded (successful defence of the assured shipowner)[118].

Limitation of liability of the shipowner according to the value of his vessel is regulated by articles 84 – 106 of the Code (KINΔ) and articles 278 – 279 of the Hellenic Commercial Law. The insurer covers the full amount of the sums paid by the assured to third parties even after the assured has limited his liability. The four – fourths liability of the underwriters is the result of the Hellenic 'all risks'

---

[114] O'May, p. 239.

[115] Hodges, p. 322. Also, Bennett, p. 239.

[116] This provision of law is *not* ius cogens. The parties of the marine insurance policy may agree that the underwriter is not liable under article 269(2) of the Code (KINΔ).

[117] The law does not state 'damages paid by the assured'. However, in practice (as we explain in paragraph dd. below) it is said that in Hellenic marine insurance the assured owner of the vessel recovers from the underwriter sums for damages that he has actually paid to third parties in the aftermath of a collision between vessels. Papapolitis, p. 207.

[118] Papapolitis, pp. 236 – 237.

principle[119]. This is a significant difference between the Code and the English collision liability clause.

bb. Upper limit to the liability of the underwriter

Article 269(2) of the Code has the significance that, if no special agreement is present in the policy, the underwriter is legally bound to cover the collision damages paid by the assured to third parties[120].

However, the underwriter is legally liable in respect of up to 100% of the insured value of the vessel insured including damages and legal costs paid by the assured in a collision case. This is the law because the insurance of the vessel contains the insurance of the shipowner's liability ('all risks' principle)[121].

The assured has, therefore, two options: first, he may agree for a special insured value in respect of the insurance of collision liability 'annexed' to the insurance of the vessel against other maritime perils[122]. Or, he may sign an independent insurance contract covering his liability against third parties[123].

The upper limit of the liability of the underwriter is then 100% of the insured value of the vessel insured (if the vessel has been a total loss) plus 100% of the insured value of the 'annexed' insured collision liability of the assured. This is the upper limit of the underwriter's liability, if there has been a special agreement. If there has been no special agreement, then the insurer is liable for all damages that the assured has paid[124], namely up to 100% of the insured value of the vessel insured. This does not arise in practice.

cc. Scope of the damages recoverable.

Article 269(2) of the Code (KINΔ) provides that 'the insurer is liable for all damages that the ship is obliged to pay to third parties'. There is no expressed distinction between damages arising in tort or in contract. However, the closer observation of the texts of the legal authors leads us to the conclusion that the damages arising in contract are not, in principle, recoverable from the underwriter under article 269(2) of the Code (KINΔ). The authors use the term 'responsibility' which in Hellenic legal terms mainly refers to liability arising in tort. If this term is used to describe liability arising in contract, the courts or the authors always make special reference to it by expressed terms. The wording and the substance of article 269(2) of the Code (KINΔ) points towards the direction that only damages in tort are recoverable. Such interpretation operates in

---

[119] This principle is analysed in Chapter B of this Part of the present text.

[120] Skouloudis, p. 384.

[121] Papapolitis, p. 127.

[122] Argyriadis, p. 115.

[123] P & I Associations in Hellas often cover the insurance of collision liability of the owner of the vessel. Doukas, p. 151.

[124] Skouloudis, p. 384.

favour of the insurer who already finds himself in a difficult position as he must cover all damages.

The damages for which an indemnity is granted under article 269(2) of the Code (ΚΙΝΔ) are all damages that the vessel is responsible to pay for[125]:

- loss of or damage to any other vessel or property thereon;
- delay to or loss of use of any other vessel or property thereon;
- salvage of any other vessel or property thereon *irrespective* of the salvage result[126];
- removal or disposal of obstructions and wrecks;
- any real or personal property on the insured vessel (in tort);
- the cargo or other property on the insured vessel (in tort).

Special clauses which exclude the liability of the underwriters are permitted under article 269(2) of the Code (ΚΙΝΔ) (usually in relation to cargo on the insured vessel) because the article does not settle *ius cogens*. Articles 173, 200 and 281 and 288 of the Hellenic Civil Code (AK) operate in such way that the courts may decide whether a specific exclusion is unfair and, consequently, illegal and void[127].

dd. Prerequisites for the application of article 269(2) of the Code (ΚΙΝΔ)

(i) *Any sums paid by the Assured*

The insurer is obliged to restore only the damages that the assured has actually paid[128] [129]. This is a legal principle based on the interpretation of the wording of article 269(2) of the Code (ΚΙΝΔ). If the shipowner becomes bankrupt, the insurer is not liable against third parties[130] [131].

(ii) *Obliged*

The meaning of 'obliged' in article 269(2) of the Code (ΚΙΝΔ) is the same as 'legally liable' under the English collision liability clause[132]. Article 235 of the Code (ΚΙΝΔ) expressly states that if the collision is the result of *force majeure*, inevitable accident or there is doubt about its causes, damages shall be borne by

---

[125] Papapolitis, pp. 224, 271, 272.
[126] Skantzakis, p.200.
[127] Argyriadis, p.117.
[128] N. 116.
[129] This a different provision from the respective provision in motor vehicle insurance. In Hellas, the third party may bring an action directly against the insurer as article 10(1) of Law 489 /1976. Also, Hatzinikolaou, pp. 49 – 69; Kiantos, p. 309; Kritikou, p. 342.
[130] Papapolitis, p. 207.
[131] In Hellenic law, there is no equivalent to the English Third Parties (Rights against Insurers) Act 1930.
[132] Paragraph a., dd., (ii) in this Chapter.

those who have suffered them[133]. However, the wording of article 269(2) of the Code (ΚΙΝΔ) does not state 'assured legally liable' (as it is in the English collision liability clause) but it refers to the 'obligation of the vessel'. Obligation of the vessel means liability of the assured owner of the vessel (article 84 of the Code (ΚΙΝΔ)).

ee. Single liability

Single liability is the basic method of calculation of the indemnity in respect of collision liability between shipowners themselves and between shipowners and underwriters. This method is based on admiralty rules. Cross – liabilities may operate only if there is a special agreement in the policy[134].

ff. Exclusions

Article 269(2) of the Code (ΚΙΝΔ) provides that the insurer is not obliged to indemnify the assured owner of the vessel for collision damages paid to third parties relating to harm to the body or health. An expressed opposite agreement is permitted[135].

The reason for this exclusion is that the insurance of the vessel (which includes insurance of collision liability) cannot include life insurance which is the object of social or private insurance[136]. For passengers of vessels operating between the Hellenic Ports, life insurance is compulsory and the price of the ticket embraces the respective premium[137].

The remaining issues are the same *mutatis mutandis* as analysed in the light of the United Kingdom law. Motor vehicle insurance differs from marine insurance in the same way as it has been already explained[138] [139]. Collision liability relates also to pollution liability. In Hellas, the insurance of the vessel against pollution liability is compulsory. This means that, in principle, the insurer does cover pol-

---

[133] This is the adoption of article 2 of the Brussels Convention. For the application of articles 235-239 of the Code by the Hellenic courts in collision cases see Piraeus Court of Appeal 682 / 2004, Review of Maritime Law (ΕΝΔ) 32 (2004) 434.

[134] Papapolitis, pp. 250 – 257. For the issue of collision and calculation of damages see Areios Pagos (ΑΠ) 1246 / 2003, Review of Maritime Law 32 (2004) 1.

[135] Skouloudis, p. 384.

[136] Kiantos, p. 105.

[137] Articles 1, 2 and 3 of the Presidential Decree 91 /1979.

[138] Paragraph a., ff., (iv).

[139] We refer here to two interesting judgments of the Athens Court of Appeal (ΕφΑθ) 4326 /1985, 37 ΕΕΔ 113 and 4936 /1985, 26 ΕλλΔικ 958. In both cases it was held that article 26(4) of the Administrative Decision of the Ministry of Commerce violated article 6(5) of Law 489 /1976. Therefore, article 26(4) is void. (*Lex superioris* means that Law is superior to Ministerial Decisions and Constitution is superior to Law). In consequence, the law in motor vehicle insurance is that the insurer is legally liable to cover the liability of the assured for damages to pavements and house yards. This is opposed to the non-cover of liability for damages to dock walls in marine insurance (as we have already said in Chapter B, paragraph c.).

lution liability of the owner of the colliding vessel. This refers to specific types of vessels[140].

c. Comparison

In both legal systems the underwriter is liable for the sum or sums paid by the assured owner of the insured vessel to third parties after a collision between vessels occurred. In English law the rule is that the insurer is liable for three – fourths of the sum paid by the assured, whilst in Hellenic law the rule is that the insurer covers the full amount paid by the assured, except there is an opposite agreement. In English law, the rule is settled by the collision liability clause. On the contrary, in Hellenic law, article 269(2) of the Code (KINΔ) settles the respective rule. This means that, if there is no special agreement in the policy, that rule bounds both the underwriter and the assured. The P & I Associations play a significant role, too. In the United Kingdom, the P & I Associations cover the remaining one – fourth that the insurers do not cover under the collision liability clause. In Hellas, cover (the only excluded liability, namely) loss of life or personal injury or illness (harm to the body or health) in consequence of collisions provided that the shipowner is not negligent and that loss of life or personal injury is not covered in the policy[141].

Under the English collision liability clause the insurer is liable in respect of up to 175% of the insured value of the vessel insured, whereas under Hellenic law the insurer covers 100% of the insured value of the vessel insured in collision including all the damages paid by the assured. If there is a special agreement (this is what actually happens in practice), the underwriter covers 100% of the insured value of the vessel insured (for a total loss of the vessel insured) plus 100% of the insured value of the liability insured 'annexed' to the insurance of the vessel (or of the independent liability insured, if there is a separate policy).

A further difference between the two legal systems is that under Hellenic law the damages paid by the assured to third parties which are recoverable from the underwriter are wider in scope than those covered under the United Kingdom collision liability clause. 'All damages' is related to the 'all risks' principle in Hellenic law. There is, however, the prerequisite under both legal systems that the assured actually paid sum or sums to third parties. This is expressly required in the English collision liability clause and it is not stated in the Hellenic provision but the interpretation of the article 269(2) of the Code (KINΔ) leads the legal authors to accept the same required prior payment as in the United Kingdom. Also, the English Third Parties (Rights against the Insurers) Act 1930 has no

---

140 Article 1 of Law 314 /1976 adopted article VII of the International Convention on Civil Liability for Oil Pollution Damages. This refers to vessels carrying more than 2, 000 tons of oil inbulk as cargo. Argyriadis (p. 115) and Skouloudis (p. 384) state that such pollution insurance is compulsory without mentioning other details.

141 Articles 1 and 9 of Decree 16560 /1938.

equivalent Law or Decree in Hellas where it stands that the insurer is not liable to third parties in collision claims if the assured became bankrupt.

The only exclusion in Hellenic law relates to what the insurer covers in respect of damages paid by the assured to third parties in consequence of collision between vessels is 'harm to the body or health'. For example, damages paid by the assured for removal of wrecks are recoverable in Hellenic law, but they are not recoverable under the United Kingdom law as they fall within the exclusion clause 8.4.1 of the collision liability clause (cl 8 of the ITCH (95)).

In general, we may draw the conclusion that the protection of the assured owner of the vessel insured is wider in Hellenic marine insurance law because the underwriters are liable for all damages (four – fourths liability) and they are not liable only for damages paid by the assured to third parties for life or personal injury claims in consequence of a collision.

PART II
ABANDONMENT

A. General

If the insured vessel collides with any other vessel or object, the consequence may be that the insured vessel or the colliding vessel becomes an actual total loss[142]. Therefore, if the collision was the proximate cause of the actual total loss, the underwriter of each of the vessels shall indemnify the assured in respect of such loss.

If the insured vessel or the colliding vessel (or cargo) is so damaged, that it is against the financial interests of the assured to recover for the damage and become afterwards responsible to repair the subject – matter insured, the assured has a legal option. He may treat such loss as if it were an actual total loss and the insurer shall, in consequence, indemnify the assured for the 'as if' total loss. Section 60 of the Act defines such loss as 'constructive total loss'[143].

If the insured vessel became a constructive total loss (because of collision or any other peril insured against), the assured may be indemnified for a total loss only if he exercises the right to abandonment by giving notice of abandonment to the underwriters[144]. These legal aspects are the objects of our comparative analysis between the United Kingdom and the Hellenic marine insurance law.

B. The right of the assured to abandon the subject – matter insured

a. United Kingdom marine insurance law

The right[145] of the assured to abandon the subject – matter insured to the underwriter arises only if there has been a constructive total loss of the subject –

---

[142] Section 57(1) of the Act defines actual total loss: 'Where the subject – matter insured is destroyed, or so damaged as to cease to be a thing of the kind insured, or where the assured is irretrievably deprived thereof, there is an actual total loss'. A vessel sank in deep water after a collision is simple to consider as an actual total loss (Goodacre, p. 659). The strict application of '*irretrievable deprivation*' is explained by Bennett (p. 364) with reference to common law.

[143] These legal aspects are dealt with in depth in this Part of the text. We say here in advance that the concept 'constructive total loss' does not legally exist in Hellas.

[144] The effect of abandonment is also discussed. We would like to mention that the comparison in this Part of the text seems to be solid because we compare English and Hellenic statutory provisions, something that it was not always the case in Part I. In any case, abandonment of the ship because of a collision or other reason is different from the abandonment of the ship in marine insurance law terms. For example, on 24th of April, 2001, nine (9) Greek seamen abandoned the ship "Macedonia 1" of Greek flag because she sank of an unknown reason; see Athens News Agency, *Nine seamen*. This "actual" abandonment differs from the "legal" abandonment, which is the subject matter of the analysis that follows.

[145] This has the meaning that the assured is not obliged to abandon the subject – matter insured to the insurer. The assured may treat the constructive total loss (defined in section 60 of the Act and below in the text) as a partial loss (section 61 of the Act).

matter insured. A constructive total loss is a total loss for the purposes of marine insurance law. The difference between actual and constructive total loss is that in the latter case the damage is repairable. However, it is not always easy to say whether a loss is an actual or constructive total loss[146]. The Act and the common law settles five types of constructive total loss[147].

(1) The first relates to any insured subject – matter (ship, goods or freight) that has been 'reasonably abandoned'. 'Reasonably abandoned' means that the master and crew left the ship with the intention of never returning[148]. In *Bradley*[149] the master sent a telegram to the owners saying that the ship had been sunk by a submarine. The master and crew were compelled to leave the ship but she was salved. The House of Lords held that there had been no abandonment of the ship by the master and crew without any intention of returning to her. In such case, no right of the assured to abandon arises[150].

---

[146] Schmitthoff (p. 529) states that the leading case in the issue is *Roux* (1836) 3 Bing 266. Abinger LJ said: 'In all these cases (unnavigable ship…), if a prudent man, not insured, would decline any further expense in prosecuting an adventure, the termination of which will probably never be successfully accomplished, a party insured may, for his own benefit, as well as that of underwriter, treat the case as one of total loss, and demand the full sum insured'.

[147] Section 60 provides as follows. (1) Subject to any express provision in the policy, there is a constructive total loss where the subject – matter insured is reasonably abandoned on account of its actual total loss appearing to be unavoidable or because it could not be preserved from actual total loss without an expenditure which would exceed its value when the expenditure had been incurred. (2) In particular, there is a constructive total loss (i) Where the assured is deprived of the possession of his ship or goods by a peril insured against, and (a) it is unlikely that he can recover the ship or goods, as the case may be, or (b) the cost of recovering the ship or goods, as the case may be, would exceed their value when recovered; or (ii) In the case of damage to a ship, where she is so damaged by a peril insured against that the cost of repairing the damage would exceed the value of the ship when repaired. In estimating the cost of repairs, no deduction is to be made in respect of general average contributions to those repairs payable by other interests, but account is to be taken of the expense of future salvage operations and of any future general average contributions to which the ship would be liable if repaired; or (iii) In the case of damage to goods, where the cost of repairing the damage and forwarding the goods to their destination would exceed their value on arrival. See Appendix I. *The first type* of constructive total loss in section (60) (unavoidable actual total loss, reasonable abandonment) refers to the abandonment made by the master or the crew (the master is responsible to take the final decision). Such abandonment has nothing to do with the abandonment in marine insurance.

[148] Hodges, p. 366.

[149] (1919) AC 16.

[150] Brett LJ in *Kaltenbach* (1878) 3 CPD 467, 470 – 471 said that such right (to abandonment) is not peculiar to marine insurance law. Gauci (in Thomas) (p. 202) states that the notion of *constructive total loss* is arguably an *exclusive* feature of the law of marine insurance. Also, he states (p. 203) that although abandonment is a consequence of payment for a total loss in every contract of indemnity, *notice* of abandonment is *exclusive* to marine insurance (notice of abandonment – *notice* is discussed in the next Chapter). Also, Colinvaux, p. 139.

(2) The second applies only to ship or goods and it is on deprivation of possession of the subject – matter insured (section 60(2)(i)).
(3) The third is concerned with damage to ship (and costs of repair exceeding its value when repaired) (section 60(2)(ii).
(4) The fourth is on damage to goods (and costs of repairing and forwarding to their destination exceeding their value on arrival) (section 60(2)(iii).
(5) The fifth has been settled by common law. In the *Sanday Case*[151] a cargo of linseed oil was sent to Germany to be sold. By reason of illegality, the goods were prevented from being carried to their proper destination. The adventure of carrying the cargo to its destination became in law a serious offence. The goods themselves were unharmed and in the actual possession of the assured. The House of Lords held that there was a constructive total loss, there was 'a destruction of the contemplated adventure' in the words of Lord Atkinson[152].

The main legal issues in this Chapter are the following.

First, there is a constructive total loss only if the deprivation of possession of or the damage to the subject – matter insured has been *proximately* caused[153] by a peril insured against (section 60(2)(i) – (ii)). Section 60(1) and section 60(2)(iii) does not refer to the cause of the loss or damage. In my opinion, in these sections it is implied that the loss or damage must also have been *proximately* caused by a peril insured against.

Second, there is a clear distinction between deprivation of the possession of or damage to the ship and to the goods. Also, in policies of goods 'subject – matter' under section 60(1) means[154] *voyage.* In *Rickards*[155] British cargo was on board a German vessel at the outbreak of the Second World War[156]. A constructive total loss occurred as soon as the master, in response to orders of the German Government, abandoned the *voyage* in favour of returning to Germany, thereby depriving the assured of possession of the goods. This means that the assured had the right to abandon the goods to the underwriters.

Third, there is constructive total loss only if the cost of repairing or recovering the ship or goods would exceed the value of the ship (when repaired or recovered) or of the goods (when repaired and forwarded to their destination or when recovered)[157].

---

[151] (1916) 1 AC 650, HL.
[152] (1916) 1 AC 650, 662, HL.
[153] Section 55(1) of the Act and Part I (n. 94).
[154] Hodges (p. 371) refers to common law.
[155] (1942) AC 50.
[156] For a collision between a US Navy Submarine with a Japanese Fishing Vessel in 2001 see CNN.
[157] In an unvalued policy (Part I, n. 65) the r e a l value is the value to be used in the respective sections regarding constructive total loss. In a valued policy the real value is the '*repaired* value' (section 27(4) and *Irving* (1847) 1 HL Cas 287), unless the policy otherwise provides. Cl 19.1 in the ITCH (95) and cl 17.1 in the IVCH (83) states that: 'in ascertaining whether the vessel is a constructive total loss, the *insured value* shall be taken as the repaired value'.

Fourth, *deprivation* of possession *means loss* of the 'free use and disposal' of the vessel insured. The owners of the vessel had been deprived of her free use and disposal in *The Bamburi*[158]. Their insured vessel (*The Bamburi*) had been restrained in the Shatt at Arab waterway and a skeleton crew was on board the vessel. No Iraqi presence was on her and the Iraqi or the Iranian government made no claim to her. It was held that loss of the 'free use and disposal of the vessel' was tantamount to the loss (deprivation) of possession of the subject – matter insured by a peril insured against, namely 'arrests, restraints and detainments' (now covered under the War and Strikes Clauses[159]). In *Rotch*[160] (to which *The Bamburi* refers) the insured vessels were held up by an embargo in French Ports. It was held that the plaintiffs could abandon and claim for a (constructive) total loss.

Fifth, the test in relation to unlikelihood of recovery of possession in section 60(2)(i) of the Act has created a number of difficult issues. Unlikelihood of recovery is understood 'within a reasonable time'. Such reasonable time is 12 months under the Detainment Clause (cl 3 of the IWSC Hulls – Time, Hulls – Voyage) or more, dependent on 'conjecture and speculation as to what is likely to be the outcome of a number of possible contingencies'[161]. This is important especially in political situations, such as the closure of the Suez Canal in 1967, as in practice most of deprivation of possession cases are related to war risks.

Sixth, unlikelihood differs from uncertainty because in the former there is some balance against the event[162]. The exact degree of unlikelihood is not defined in section 60(2)(i) of the Act. In *Polurrian*[163], on the outbreak of the First World War a Hellenic warship captured a ship bound from England to Constantinople. It was held that there was no constructive total loss because recovery of the deprived possession by the assured shipowners within reasonable time was not unlikely, but u n c e r t a i n. 'If[164] on the test of uncertainty the scales are l e v e l, any degree of unlikelihood would seem to shift the balance, however slightly. It is not required that the seale should spring up and kick the beam'.

Finally, unlikelihood of recovery of the deprived possession by the assured is subject to the objective test relating to the person to whom unlikelihood appears. That person is not the individual concerned (facts as known to the assured), but it is the reasonable man (true facts as then existing[165]). Otherwise it would be to

---

Hodges extensively (pp. 378 – 390) explains 'recovery' and 'repair' in the context of constructive total loss.

[158] (1982) 1 Lloyd's Rep 312.

[159] Institute War and Strikes Clauses (Cargo) – (Hulls – Time) – (Freight – Time) (*IWSC*), clause 1.2.

[160] (1795) 6 TR 413.

[161] Per Warrington J in *Polurrian* (1915) 1 KB 1922; All ER 116; 20 Com Cas 152.

[162] N. 22 and the text following it.

[163] (1915) 1 KB 1922; All ER 116; 20 Com Cas 152.

[164] Wright LJ in *Forest* (1941) 70 LlLRep 173, 191.

[165] *Marstrand* (1937) 1 All ER 158.

hold that 'the insurance had been effected, not against loss, but against bad news'[166].

b. Hellenic marine insurance law

The right[167] of the assured to abandon the subject – matter insured to the underwriter arises only if one of the four cases occurs under article 281 of the Code (ΚΙΝΔ). The notion 'constructive total loss' does not exist[168] in Hellenic marine insurance law[169].

There are only[170] five cases where the assured may abandon the vessel, the cargo or the freight insured.

(1) If the ship was lost or is not capable of navigation and it is not possible[171] to be repaired (article 281(a)).

(2) If the cost for the repair and the restoration of the damaged ship exceed the three – fourths of the insured value of the vessel insured (article 281(b)).

---

[166] Hodges, p. 376.

[167] The assured is not obliged in Hellenic law to abandon. He may not abandon and treat the loss as partial loss. (The same is stated in n. 4 concerning the United Kingdom marine insurance law). However, it is most of the times preferable for him to abandon and claim for a total loss. This is the justified reason (protection of financial interests of the assured shipowner – Chapter A) why the Code (ΚΙΝΔ) introduces the institution of abandonment in marine insurance law. (Kiantos (82), p. 157).

[168] Article 280 of the Code (ΚΙΝΔ) provides as follows. 'The assured has the right to abandon to the underwriter the subject – matter insured and to claim for a total loss, in the cases and under the conditions of the following articles' (articles 281 – 288). Article 281 of the Code (ΚΙΝΔ) states the following. 'The abandonment of the vessel or the cargo or the freight, may be exercised only when a) the ship, in consequence of a maritime casualty, is lost or is no more capable of navigation and any repair of it is not possible, b) the cost of refloating, repairing and restoration of the ship in a condition where it may continue navigating, exceed three – fourths of the insured value or when the repair is not attainable on the place of the casualty, nor is it possible the transportation of the repair means thereon or the towage of the ship to port where it may be repaired, γ) (c)) from the last news for the ship three months have passed for machine – operated ships, or five months for sailing ships, therefore the peril is considered to have occurred the day following the day when the last news was heard and δ) (d)) the ship is captured or detained (hindered) by order of foreign power, and the insurance policy cover the war risks.

[169] Abandonment is peculiar to Hellenic law of marine insurance. Doukas, p. 155; Kiantou – Pampouki, p. 81. The opposite is stated in n. 9 as regards English law.

[170] This is an exhaustive enumeration (same in section 60 of the Act, Hodges, p. 370). In Hellenic law, this probably means that *ius cogens* is settled (no opposite agreement is permitted). Kiantos (82)(p.182) argues that article 280 of the Code (ΚΙΝΔ) sets ius cogens. An opposite view has held by Piraeus Court of Fist Instance (ΠΠΠειρ) 201 /1921, 22 (ΑΒ΄) Θ 137.

[171] Today the possibility that the vessel cannot be repaired is very low given the progress of new technology. Therefore, the third case (under article 281(b)) is of great importance. Argyriadis, p. 124.

(3) If the repair is not attainable on the place of the casualty, not is it possible the towage of the ship to port where it may be repaired (article 281(b)).
(4) If there has been no news for three or five months for the machine – operated or the sailing ship respectively (article 281(c)).
(5) If the ship is captured or detained by order of foreign power, provided that the insurance policy covers war risks (article 281(d)).

The main legal issues are the following.

First, the right to abandonment arises only when the loss or damage has been proximately caused by a peril insured against. This is expressly stated in article 281(c) and (d) of the Code (KINΔ). It is also implied in article 281(a) and (b)[172].

Second, there is no distinction between (deprivation of possession) loss of or damage to the vessel and the cargo. The assured may abandon the vessel, the cargo or the freight to the underwriter if the vessel insured was lost or damaged. The loss of cargo or the damage to the cargo does not affect the right of the assured to abandon the cargo insured[173]. This is severely criticised by the Hellenic legal authors[174]. For example, it is argued that it is right that the abandonment of the freight insured depends on the loss of the vessel insured[175].

However, it is wrong that the abandonment of the cargo insured depends on the loss of the vessel insured. Firstly, if only the cargo insured has been captured by a foreign power (for instance, cargo on a ship neutral to the foreign power) for war purposes, the assured cannot abandon the cargo insured because the ship was not lost or damaged. Secondly, if the vessel was damaged but the cargo insured has been remained untouched, the assured may abandon the cargo insured. Sarlis[176] argues that in this second case the assured may abandon the cargo insured only if one of the cases of article 281 of the Code (KINΔ) occurred p l u s it is impossible to forward the cargo within reasonable time. Reasonable time depends on the specific circumstances and the nature of the cargo (seasonal goods, and so forth).

Third, the right to abandonment arises if the cost of repair and restoration of the damaged vessel insured exceeds the three – fourths of the insured value of the vessel insured. Moreover, if the repair is not possible on the place of the casualty or the transportation of the means of repair is impossible, then the right to abandonment also arises. This latter case is separated from that settled in article 281(a) (impossible to repair)[177].

---

[172] Rokas I., p. 182; Skouloudis, p. 400.
[173] Stamelos, pp. 166-167.
[174] Argyriadis, p. 123; Kiantos, p.321.
[175] Sarlis, pp. 159 – 160.
[176] Sarlis, p. 167.
[177] N. 29. If the transportation of means of repair on the place of the casualty is technically possible but the cost is too high, the first case of article 281(b) applies (the three – fourths test) and not the second (which does not require the three – fourths test). The second applies only if it is not possible at all for anyone to bring means of repair on the place of the casualty.

Fourth, loss means total loss and this includes not only material disaster of the vessel insured but also that it is impossible for the assured to exercise his rights stemming from his ownership on her[178]. For example, this may happen if pirates violently capture the vessel insured. If the insured vessel is captured by order of foreign power, the right to abandonment is based on article 281(d). In such case, it is required an increased uncertainty whether the peril insured against[179] has actually occurred[180].

Fifth, article 282 of the Code (ΚΙΝΔ) provides that it is permitted for the assured to exercise his right to abandon the vessel insured only after 3 months[181] have passed since the notification[182] that the vessel insured was captured or detained by order of foreign power[183] (article 281(d)). Although there is a legal time *minimum* for the assured to exercise his right to abandonment, there is no legal *maximum* (in article 282) after which the assured is not permitted to exercise such right. Articles 283 and 288 give two rules relating to time. The *maximum* is three months after the three months of article 282 have passed. Also, the insurer may set a time limit to the assured[184]. These aspects are also dealt with in the next Chapter (notice of abandonment).

Finally, article 281(c) provides that the right of the assured to abandon the subject matter insured (vessel, cargo or freight) arises, if no news[185] was heard for three or five months (machine – operated or sailing ships respectively). The justified reason for this provision is not only that there is uncertainty[186] whether the peril insured against has occurred or not but also that the commercial transactions operate fast and this is how the marine insurance contractual relationship between the insurer and the assured must operate, or else be terminated. In the rare case where there is no news for the vessel insured but there is news for the

---

[178] Sarlis, p. 163.

[179] This is different from the English unlikelihood.

[180] Kiantos (82), p. 171.

[181] Doukas (p. 155) emphatically says: ‘it is compulsory that 3 months shall pass’.

[182] It is not specified h o w this notification may be communicated or what notification is. A similar issue (news) is discussed below in the present paragraph.

[183] Foreign power means any government or r e b e l s of a foreign country. ‘Foreign’ refers to the flag of the insured vessel. Kiantos (82), p. 259. The capture or detainment must relate to the foreign war aims and not to any other aim (for instance, creditors of the vessel convinced the foreign power to detain the vessel insured for their own private purposes). Also, it is of no significance for the purposes of marine insurance (and the right to abandonment) whether the order is legal or if it is not the result of a competent authority. The right to abandonment still arises. Kiantos (82), p. 323.

[184] If the settled time passes, then the assured can only claim for a partial loss.

[185] News may be sent by the master or crew by letter or telegram. News may also be sent by residents of an island or a city by the sea who saw the vessel insured. Skantzakis, p. 15.

[186] This differs from the English requirement of ‘unlikelihood of recovery of possession’. Also, n. 36.

cargo[187], it is argued that article 281(c) should not provide for the right of the assured to abandon the cargo insured.

c. Comparison

The right of the assured to abandon the subject – matter insured to the underwriter is recognized under both the English and Hellenic law of marine insurance. The assured may claim for an actual total loss or for a partial loss. This is legally valid only if the loss of or damage to the subject – matter insured (the vessel insured in Hellenic terms) occurred because of a peril insured against.

A striking difference between the two legal orders is that constructive total loss is an unknown legal term for the purposes of the Hellenic Code (ΚΙΝΔ). Furthermore, the assured in Hellenic law may abandon the vessel, the cargo or the freight insured in cases where the vessel is lost, damaged or captured. This highlights the right choice of the United Kingdom Legislator who clearly distinguished damage to (or loss of) the cargo insured and the consequent right of the assured to abandon the cargo insured from damage to the vessel insured and the respective consequent right of the assured.

Another difference refers to the criterion of how the repair is calculated in case of damage to the subject – matter (vessel in Hellenic terms) insured. First, under section 60 of the Act the real value is taken into account, albeit in practice the United Kingdom policies (cl 19.1 of the ITCH (95), cl 17.1 of the IVCH (83)) provide that the insured value of the subject – matter insured shall be taken into account. This latter is the legal requirement under article 281(b) of the Code (ΚΙΝΔ). Second, the cost of recovery or repair shall exceed the value of the insured subject – matter when repaired (insured vessel) or repaired and forwarded (insured cargo). This is the law in the United Kingdom under section 60 of the Act. On the contrary, the Hellenic provision (article 281(b)) the respective expenses (which include refloating, repairs and restoration of the vessel insured to navigation) shall exceed three – fourths of the insured value of the vessel insured.

In other words, the assured in Hellenic law may abandon the subject – matter insured by applying an easier test than the assured applies in English law. This is true regarding at least the abandonment of the vessel insured. It is also remarkable that in the collision marine insurance the two legal orders take the 'opposite' view.

In United Kingdom law the underwriter covers the three – fourths of the damages paid to third parties by the assured in respect of his collision liability, whereas in Hellenic law the underwriter covers all the damages paid to third parties by the assured in respect of his collision liability.

This 'converted' difference may turn to be a similarity in the sense that the assured is widely protected in Hellenic law and the underwriter is benefited in

[187] The relevant issues in relation to abandonment of cargo insured dependent on loss of the vessel have already been analysed above in the present paragraph (*second*).

United Kingdom law (*for instance, higher test of criterion of value for calculation of constructive total loss in section 60 of the Act for the assured*), if we compare the two systems between themselves. It is not easy to say in theory whether the one or the other law is better or right. However, the assured or the underwriter would logically choose the national law which provides more benefits for him. In practice, many other factors may influence their final choice of law.

Unlikelihood is also an unknown legal requirement in Hellenic marine insurance.

Also, the recovery of the ship insured must be unlikely (or deeply uncertain) within a reasonable time. In United Kingdom law, reasonable time is at least 12 months under clause 3 of the IWSC (Hulls – Time, Hulls – Voyage). In Hellenic law, the reasonable time is 3 or 5 months but it does not refer to unlikelihood. It refers to whether the insured peril has occurred. For example, the law sets the assumption that the peril has occurred if 3 or 5 months have passed since the last news was heard from a machine – operated or a sailing ship. Further legal discussion over uncertainty stops to the statement that increased uncertainty is legally required. This uncertainty does not refer to whether the assured may recover his deprived possession of the vessel insured but to whether the insured peril has occurred. Again, the English requirements are more: deprivation of possession by a peril insured against a n d unlikelihood of recovering the deprived possession of the assured. In Hellas, if it is settled that the peril insured against has occurred, then the right to abandonment arises (article 281(a), (c) and *m a i n l y* (d)).

C. The notice of abandonment

a. United Kingdom marine insurance law

If the right of the assured to abandon the subject – matter insured to the underwriters arises (a type of constructive total loss under section 60 of the Act), the assured may exercise such right by giving notice of abandonment (*notice*). If he fails to do so, the loss can only be treated as a partial loss[188].

The reason behind the requirement of notice to underwriters is easily understood. It is necessary in order that the underwriters shall be entitled, if they so wish, to take over whatever remains of the subject – matter insured, and enable them to take steps, if they are so minded, to protect their interests. In *Vacuum*[189] Atkin LJ said: 'The object of notice is twofold. First of all, to enable the underwriters to exercise as soon as they can the care over the goods which otherwise are under the control of the assured; secondly, to prevent the assured from continuing to have an option over the underwriters, so that he may say that the

[188] Section 62(1) of the Act sets this rule in accordance with section 61 (*right* of the assured to abandon).

[189] (1926) 25 LlLRep 546, CA.

goods are or are not their property in accordance with the eventual state of the goods, and sometimes in accordance with the *rise or fall of the market* for such goods'.

In practice[190], a fairly standardised wording has developed, so that on receipt of advice from the assured the broker[191] will prepare a letter in a form similar to the following[192].

* * *

To the underwriters concerned *Date*

Gentlemen,

VESSEL AND ACCIDENT

By the instructions of the Assured, we hereby abandon to you their interest in this Vessel so far as may be concerned your subscriptions on Hull and Machinery *etc* valued at __________
and we claim thereon Total Loss.

Yours faithfully,

____

In the event of your declining to accept abandonment, it shall be understood that you agree to the Assured being placed in the same position as if a writ had been issued this day for the amount of your subscriptions.

* * *

aa. Necessary notice of abandonment

There are three cases (*apart from the one in practice relating to cargo insured*[193]) in which the assured may legally claim for a constructive total loss without giving notice of abandonment[194]. First, notice is unnecessary where, at the time when the assured receives information of the loss, there would be no possibility of benefit to the insurer if notice were given to him (section 62(7) of

[190] In practice, formal notice on cargo is r a r e l y necessary. O'May, p. 436.

[191] The broker is the agent of the assured and owes him a combination of fiduciary and contractual duties. Bennett, p. 80.

[192] The presented sample of notice is taken from Goodacre, p. 665.

[193] N. 47.

[194] In the case of an actual total loss no notice of abandonment need be given. Section 57(2) of the Act. In such case notice is considered to be a mere '*idle ceremony*'. Arnould, p. 1044.

the Act). In *Rankin*[195] a ship was chartered in the United Kingdom to bring a cargo from Calcutta to London, and a policy was effected on that homeward freight but to cover the voyage from Clyde to New Zealand. Thirty days after arrival there, a constructive total loss of ship occurred during the currency of that policy, as the owner was n o t bound in these circumstances to repair his ship (and did not do so). There was a total loss of the homeward freight and nothing to abandon, so that notice would have been unmeaning and was held unnecessary. Blackburn J said[196]: 'If there was nothing (the underwriters) could do, no notice is required'.

Ivamy[197] extensively refers to the respective English judgments and arrives to the following conclusion. 'Although the rule is established that, where no benefit can accrue to the insurer from a notice of abandonment, such notice need not be given, it is still desirable, and indeed safer, for an assured to give notice in a l l cases where he can possibly do so, whether the policy is on freight, goods or ship. For if there is a possibility of the insurer deriving an advantage from the notice, it will be dangerous for the assured to fail to give it'. This was the case in *Vacuum*[198]. The insurance was on petroleum in tins, being carried from Alexandria to Cyprus in a vessel which was wrecked on the Syrian coast. A large proportion of tins floated ashore, and those that were capable of being made merchantable were forwarded to Tripoli, being sold there. Although underwriters could have derived no further benefit, Bankes LJ pronounced on section 67(2) of the Act by saying: 'When the statute speaks of no possibility of benefit, it does not mean that in the events which have happened the underwriter would have been no better off'. Although the assured apparently acted quite prudently in disposing of salved cargo, it was held that notice should have been given to cargo underwriters.

Second, notice is unnecessary if the insurer[199] has waived[200] the right to it. Finally, notice is unnecessary where the insurer has re – insured his risk[201]. In *Uzielli*[202] it was held that upon a constructive total loss of ship no notice need be given by the original underwriters to underwriters on a policy of re – insurance.

In all (other) cases of constructive total loss, notice is required to be given by the assured to the underwriter[203]. The assured exercises his right to abandonment

---

[195] (1873) LR 6, HL.
[196] (1873) LR 6, 124, HL.
[197] Pp. 382 – 385.
[198] (1926) 25 LlLRep 546, CA.
[199] Section 62(8) of the Act.
[200] A waiver of the right to notice can only be established by plain evidence. Arnould, p. 1053. A waiver may be either express or implied. Waiver will be implied where a demand made by the assured is followed by a payment of a total loss by the insurer. Ivamy, p. 392. Also, Hodges, pp. 399 – 400.
[201] Section 62(9) and section 9(1) of the Act.
[202] (1884) 15 QBD 11, CA.
[203] Section 62(1) of the Act.

by giving notice of abandonment. Notice is an essential prerequisite (*condition precedent*) for the assured to claim for a constructive total loss and it is not an essential ingredient of a constructive total loss. This has been illustrated in *The Robertson* by Lord Porter[204]:

'A constructive total loss may exist, but if the assured wishes to take advantage of it he must give notice of abandonment'.

bb. Who may give notice of abandonment

Notice of abandonment can only be given by or upon the authority[205] of the owner of the interest. The test of ownership in such a case and for the purpose is whether the person who abandons is in such a position in reference to the interest abandoned that he can effectually assign it[206]. A mere deposit of the policy of insurance with a bank (by way of security for a loan, which in itself conveyed no interest in the ship insured) gave no implied authority to the pledgee[207] to give notice of abandonment[208].

If the policy covers various interests under separately valuations, one or all of the assured may abandon each of their respective interests without notice to, or the concurrence of, the assured on other interests[209].

cc. To whom notice of abandonment must be given

Notice of abandonment must be given to the insurers themselves[210] or to their authorised agent[211]. In practice, the broker, on behalf of the assured, presents to the insurer the formal letter presented above. Moreover, the Newcastle 1995 P & I Rulebook provides: 'In the event of ... a constructive total loss, the Association shall ... be entitled to request the Member concerned to abandon the ship *to the Association or to such other person* (*including the world at large*) as the Association shall nominate'. This Rulebook requires that the notice must be given to the P & I Club, a third party to the contract of insurance or the world at large.

---

204 (1939) AC 371, 393, HL.

205 The master is agent of the assured until abandonment. By abandonment he becomes the agent of the underwriter. Arnould, p. 1076. Abandonment of the subject – matter insured means abandonment of the insured interest in the subject – matter insured.

206 *Stewart* (1848) 2 HL Cas 159.

207 Pledge or pawn is an item of goods transferred by the owner (pledgor or pawnor) to another (pledgee or pawnee) as security for a debt. Martin, p. 334.

208 *Jardine* (1863) 32 LJQB 132.

209 Ivamy, p.381. The author also refers to similar possibilities.

210 Sections 61, 62. Section 60 does not specify to whom the subject – matter insured must be abandoned.

211 In *Vacuum* (n. 55) Atkin LJ said: 'I do not think that Lloyd's Agents in different parts of the world are the persons who, in ordinary circumstances, have authority to receive notice of abandonment'.

dd. Form of notice of abandonment

Section 62(2) of the Act provides as follows: 'Notice of abandonment may be given in writing, or by word of mouth, or partly in writing and partly by word of mouth, and may be given in any terms which indicate the intention of the assured to abandon his insured interest in the subject – matter insured unconditionally to the insurer'. Two words are worth of our comments. First, 'any' (terms) means 'expressly or implied'. Second, 'unconditionally' means that notice shall be absolute and without any condition for the underwriters. The notice is absolute, even if the word 'abandon' is not referred[212]. However, the word 'abandon' is clearly desirable[213].

In *Curie*[214] notice of abandonment was given in the following words. 'With regard to the "Northland", we regret to say that she is a total wreck, and we have hereby to give you notice that we shall claim payment of the policies we hold against her cargo and disbursements'. It was held that this amounted to a notice of abandonment.

In *Russian Bank*[215] the owners of cargo insured it from Novorossiysk (in the Black Sea) to Falmouth. After the closure of the Dardanelles (in November 1914) the owners of the cargo insured sent a telegraph to their brokers with the following words. 'Agreeable release underwriters from all risks if underwriters will pay the difference between present value in Novorossiysk and insured value'. The Court of Appeal held that the notice of abandonment was conditional ('if underwriters will pay ...') and, therefore, the notice of abandonment was not good.

ee. When notice of abandonment need be given

The assured (owner of the interest) must give notice 'with reasonable diligence after the receipt of reliable information of the loss, but where the information is of a doubtful character the assured is entitled to a reasonable time to make inquiry'[216].

The rule is that if the information is certain, notice must be given to the underwriters immediately or promptly[217]. If the information is of a doubtful character, the assured may wait a reasonable time for more accurate information as to

---

[212] Lord Ellenborough CJ took the opposite view in *Parmeter* (1808) 1 Camp 541. The notice must include the word 'abandon' to be absolute. In practice, 'abandon' is used in notice as we have already shown in the sample (formal letter) above.

[213] Ivamy, p. 386. Also, Arnould, p. 1049. We have already mention that where notice is unnecessary, it is still d e s i r a b l e.

[214] (1869) LR 3 PC 72.

[215] (1919) 35 TLR 42.

[216] Section 62(3) of the Act. Section 88 states: '[T]he question what is reasonable is a question of fact'.

[217] Bennett, p. 355. Arnould, p. 1054. Hodges (p. 396) argues that 'an assured is not expected, on receipt of information of the loss of his ship, to react immediately to give notice of abandonment'.

the nature of the loss, or the actual extent of the damage. He then elects to abandon or not. This does not mean that the assured is permitted to delay and watch the turn of events or observe the state of the markets[218].

The older cases on the topic of timely notice give less guidance nowadays, when the speed and availability of modern communications have foreshortened the time required for making a decision[219].

In *Aldridge*[220] notice might have been given by post in 4 days after the 14 December when the fact of constructive total loss was ascertained by survey. Nevertheless, it was given on 6 January. It was held that the notice had been given too late. In *Hunt*[221] a ship was surveyed and condemned on 11 December. Notice was given on 22 December, although it might have been given on 17 December. It was held that those five days of delay was unreasonable. Therefore, the assured was entitled to recover only for a partial loss[222]. In *George Cohen*[223] an absolute battleship left Chatham in December 1922 for Germany to be broken up. After 2 or 3 days she stranded on the Dutch coast, and became a constructive total loss. In February 1923 the assured claimed for a total loss, and in April 1923 gave formal notice of abandonment. Roche J held that the claim made in February 1923 had been made within a reasonable time.

ff. Acceptance of notice of abandonment

Section 60(4) of the Act reads: 'Where notice of abandonment is properly given, the rights of the assured are not prejudiced by the fact that the insurer refuses to accept the abandonment'. The duty imposed on the assured to decide promptly on the question of abandonment imposes no corresponding obligation on the insurer who may wait to ascertain what the circumstances really are before he decides either to pay a total loss or to reject the abandonment[224].

The significance of acceptance is that the insurer thereby 'conclusively admits liability for the loss and the sufficiency of the notice'[225]. Also, where notice is accepted the abandonment is irrevocable[226]. This means that by giving notice the assured merely makes an offer which remains executory unless and until it is accepted[227].

The mere silence of the insurer after notice is not an acceptance[228]. This does not mean that 'silence of the insurer' is a refusal of acceptance. It means that 'si-

[218] *Gernon* (1815) 6 Taunt 383, 387.
[219] O'May, p. 427.
[220] (1816) 1 Stark 498.
[221] (1816) 5 M & S 47.
[222] Ivamy, p. 389.
[223] (1925) 30 Com Cas 139, KBD.
[224] Ivamy, p. 389.
[225] Section 62(6) of the Act.
[226] N. 82.
[227] *Pesquerias* (1946) 79 LlLRep 417, KBD. Hodges, p. 397; O'May, p. 429.
[228] Section 62(5) of the Act.

lence' does not constitute acceptance, so that the underwriter does not conclusively admits liability for the loss and the sufficiency of the notice.

If the insurer declines to accept the abandonment and the assured wishes to enforce his legal claim (*refusal of acceptance does not prejudice the rights of the assured*) for constructive total loss, it will be necessary for him to issue a writ against the underwriters. In practice, to avoid court fees and administrative costs, underwriters almost invariably agree in writing to put the assured in the same position as if a writ had been issued[229]. If an insurer elects to contest a claim for a constructive total loss, it is the state of affairs on the date of the writ which must govern the decision of the Court as it in *Ruys*[230] where it is illustrated the way in which circumstances can alter between the date the writ is issued and the time the trial of action commences.

In 1896 Italy was at war with Abyssinia, and an Italian cruiser (*fast warship*) captured a vessel carrying a cargo of munitions for the king of Abyssinia. Following refusal of the notice by the underwriters covering the vessel against was risks, a writ was issued. However, by the time the trial commenced peace had been declared between the two nations so that a Prize Court had released the vessel to the owners. It was held (by Collins J) that a constructive total loss had been proved on the date of the writ and the assured was entitled to recover for a total loss under the policy[231].

The acceptance of abandonment may be either express or implied from the conduct of the insurer[232]. The scope of the concept 'implied acceptance from the conduct of the insurer' is limited by the Sue and Labour Clause[233] which reads: 'Measures taken by the Assured or the Underwriters with the object of saving, protecting or recovering the subject – matter insured shall not be considered as a waiver of acceptance of abandonment or otherwise prejudice the rights of either party'.

If the underwriter accepts the abandonment, he is not entitled to withdraw the acceptance. Nevertheless, if there is a fundamental mistake of fact (mistake of law is not suffice ground[234]), the abandonment is a nullity. In *Norwich*[235] the true facts were neither known to the assured nor to the underwriter at the time the assured gave notice of abandonment. The assured were under the impression that the insured cargo of lemons had been justifiably sold off short of destination consequent on damage sustained in a c o l l i s i o n of the carrying vessel and that the lemons had become a total loss by perils insured. Underwriters settled the claim but the Privy Council held that a notice and acceptance of abandon-

[229] O'May, p.43.
[230] (1897) 2 QB 135.
[231] Also, *Marstrand* (1936) 56 LlLRep 163, 173.
[232] N. 85.
[233] Clause 11.3 of the ITCH (95) and of the IVCH (83).
[234] O'May, p. 429.
[235] (1934) AC 455.

ment based on a mistake was a nullity. The sum insured should be repaid, as the lemons had not been damaged by a peril insured against and the sale was solely because of their ripening condition due to inherent vice or delay. Lord Wright said: 'Mistake may render a notice of abandonment a nullity, so in the same way it may render an acceptance of the notice a nullity'[236].

If the assured withheld information from the underwriter[237], the acceptance of notice may be revoked by them on general grounds of mispresentation[238].

gg. The effect of abandonment

(i) Section 63(1) provides: 'Where there is a valid abandonment the insurer is entitled to take over the interest of the assured in whatever may remain of the subject – matter insured, and all proprietary rights incidental thereto'.

The reason why the underwriter is entitled to take over whatever may remain of the subject – matter insured is that the assured shall not be permitted both to receive the total loss indemnity and retain any value remaining of the subject – matter insured because this would produce *unjust enrichment* of the assured to the extent of the remaining value of the subject – matter insured. The law of marine insurance strives to avoid the assured being unjustly enriched through any recovery in excess of the measure of indemnity provided by law. A contract of marine insurance is a contract of indemnity, not a way of pure financial speculation for the assured[239].

Where there is a valid abandonment, the insurer is e n t i t l e d to take over whatever may remain of the subject – matter insured; he is n o t bound to do so. The underwriter has the option to do or not to do so. The notice of abandonment in itself does not pass any property or rights in the thing insured to the underwriter[240].

Where the insurer pays for a total loss[241] [...], he thereupon becomes entitled to take over the interest of the assured in whatever may remain of the subject – matter insured so paid for, and he is thereby subrogated to all the rights and remedies of the assured in respect of that subject – matter as from the time of the casualty causing the loss[242].

The legal rights given by abandonment are distinguished from the rights of subrogation[243]. Lord Atkin in *AG* said[244]: 'No one doubts that the underwriter on

---

236 (1934) AC 455 467.

237 O'May, p. 429.

238 Mispresentation is an untrue statement of fact by one party that induces the other party to enter inot the contract. Martin, p. 295.

239 Bennett, p. 10.

240 Scrutton CJ in *Allgemeine* (1931) 1 KB 672, 687, CA. Also, below.

241 This means either actual or constructive total loss.

242 Section 79(1) of the Act.

243 The extent of the subrogative rights has to be considered in relation to recovery of damages from a wrong – doer (for instance, in collision); gifts received by the assured; and the

hull damaged by collision and abandonment as a constructive total loss is entitled to the benefit of the right of the assured to sue the wrongdoer for the damage to hull. But he derives his right from the provisions of section 79 (of the Act), whereby he is subrogated to "all rights and remedies of the assured in and in respect of the subject – matter", very different words from "all proprietary rights incidental thereto". And it is to be noted that in respect of abandonment the rights exist on a valid abandonment, whereas in subrogation they only arise on payment'.

One further question is whether the insured property which has been validly abandoned, but has not taken over by the insurers, becomes *res nullius*[245].
In the early common law (*Simpson*[246]), property passed automatically to the insurer. The legislation (the Act) altered that law. However, the statutory law does not state whether the assured may divest himself of his interest in the insured property by a unilateral act of abandonment to the insurer or whether, pending acceptance by the insurer, he is obliged to retain his interest in such property as remains in existence, together with attendant liabilities[247].

In *Mayor* Bailhache J said[248]: 'I have refrained from expressing any opinion whether a valid notice of abandonment, unaccepted by underwriters, while it divests the owner of his property in the wreck at the same time automatically transfers the property to the underwriters. I will only say that there is a good deal to be said against this view in favour of the wreck becoming in such circumstances a *res nullius*'. In that case it was held that the owner of the vessel prior to its being abandoned was not liable for wreck removal expenses.

Hodges[249] argues that the two views expressed above are difficult to support on the ground of the wording of sections 63, 79 and 61 of the Act. If the assured was held to have been divested of ownership of the remains, it would be impossible for him to treat the loss as a partial loss. Indeed, Greer LJ in *Oceanic* said[250]: 'It does not follow that, because of notice of abandonment is given to an insurer, therefore the vessel [...] becomes what lawyers prefer to describe, using the Latin language, a *res nullius*'. The property remains in the ownership of the assured until such time as the insurer exercises his right to take over control or ownership over the abandoned property.
This appears to be the preponderant view[251].

---

right to salvage in the case of under – insurance. Hodges, p. 11. Also, Arnould, pp. 1067 – 1070.
244 (1930) 37 LlLRep 55, 61, HL.
245 Res nullius is a thing belonging to no one.
246 (1877) 3 App Cas 278, 292.
247 Bennett, pp. 351, 357.
248 (1923) 15 LlLRep 85; 28 Com Cas 367, 373.
249 Pp. 10 – 11.
250 (1934) 50 LlLRep 1, 3, CA.
251 Hodges, p. 11.

In other words[252], '*A man does not cease to own property simply by saying "I don't want"*'.

(ii) Section 63(2) of the Act provides: 'Upon the abandonment of a ship, the insurer thereof is entitled to any freight in course of being earned, and which is earned by her subsequent to the casualty causing the loss, less the expenses of earning it incurred after the casualty; and where the ship is carrying the owner's goods, the insurer is entitled to a reasonable remuneration for the carriage of them subsequent to the casualty causing the loss'. Clause 20 of the ITCH (95) provides: 'In the event of actual or constructive total loss no claim to be maid by the underwriters for freight whether notice of abandonment has been given or not'. In *Sea Insurance*[253] a vessel was engaged under a charter – party, and her owner effected separate insurances on ship and on chartered freight with different underwriters. The vessel was lost in collision before the chartered freight had been earned, and the owner abandoned to the insurers on ship. In subsequent litigation the assured recovered damages from the owners of the other ship for the loss of chartered freight, and the insurers on ship claimed to receive this from the assured. It was held that they were not entitled to do so. Arnould[254] extensively deals with other issues relating to the effect of abandonment and the freight insured.

b. Hellenic marine insurance law

If the right of the assured to abandon the subject – matter insured to the underwriter arises, the assured may exercise that right by giving notice of abandonment. Article 284 of the Code (KINΔ) states: 'The right to abandonment is exercised by declaration notified to the insurer'[255]. If the assured fails to do so, the loss can only be treated as partial loss[256].The reason behind the requirement of notice of abandonment to underwriters is that they may take over whatever remains of the subject – matter insured or raise doubts as to whether the right of abandonment has legally arisen or not[257].

aa. Necessary notice of abandonment

The assured may waive his right to abandonment before notifying the declaration (giving notice) either expressly or from conduct which implies it (for instance, if he claims for a partial loss, he cannot give notice of abandonment afterwards)[258]. In all other cases, the assured must notify his declaration.

---

[252] Gauci, p. 208.
[253] (1884) 13 QBD 706.
[254] Pp. 1065 – 1068.
[255] Giving notice is equal to notifying declaration.
[256] Skouloudis, p. 402.
[257] Argyriadis, p. 125.
[258] Skouloudis, p. 403.

bb. Who may give notice of abandonment

Only the owner of the interest can give notice of abandonment. The notice may be given by the legal representative of the owner of the interest, if the legal representative is permitted to transfer the ownership upon the subject – matter insured[259].

If the policy covers various interests under separately valuations, one or all of the assured may abandon each of their respective interests without notice to the assured on other interests[260].

cc. To whom notice of abandonment must be given

Declaration of abandonment must be notified to the insurer[261]. The best is that the notification is made directly to the insurer. It may be made to his representative but not to his agent because the agent[262] is not specifically authorised. The fact that declaration must be notified to the insurer or his representative means that it is of no legal significance if the insurer or his representative got knowledge of the contents of the declaration which has been notified to him. It is not significant if the insurer or his representative opened, for example, the letter and read the text of the declaration[263]. The notification follows the declaration. Before the notification, the assured may withdraw the declaration. After the notification to the underwriter the notified declaration of abandonment (the given notice of abandonment) is irrevocable.

Needless to say, if both parties agree, the notified declaration is revocable[264].

dd. Form of notice of abandonment

Article 284 of the Code (ΚΙΝΔ) does not specify how the notice (declaration) should be given (notified). Skantzakis[265] and Skouloudis[266] (Athenian legal authors) state that the declaration shall be in writing. The Athens Court of Appeal has decided the same[267]. On the contrary, Argyriadis[268] (Thessalonikis legal author) finds that 'nowadays there is no reason for the Hellenic law to require written declaration of abandonment contrary to the international practice'. He sup-

---

259 Skantzakis, p. 211.

260 Doukas, p. 155; Sarlis, pp. 169 – 171.

261 Article 284 of the Code (ΚΙΝΔ).

262 Kiantos (82), p. 267.

263 Kiantos (82), p. 324.

264 Kiantos (82), p. 263.

265 P. 210. Also, it is not legally required that the declaration shall include the word 'abandon'. It is suffice that the *voluntas* for abandonment is obvious. The notified declaration is proved by all evidence, but not by witness. Athens Court of First Instance (ΕφΑθ) 9425 /1966, 17 (ΙΖ΄) ΕΕΔ, 414.

266 P. 402.

267 Athens Court of Appeal (ΕφΑθ) 1011 /1968, 19 (ΙΘ΄) ΕΕΔ 403.

268 P. 125.

ports such view by making special reference to section 62(2) of the English Marine Insurance Act 1906.

Kiantos[269] argues that 'the declaration may be notified in writing or orally because article 284 does not specify the issue. However, it should be better if the declaration were in writing because the doubts over its validity can be decreased'[270].

ee. When notice of abandonment need be given

Article 283 of the Code (KINΔ) reads: 'The right to abandonment is exercised within a time – limit of three months, which starts running the next day of the day when the casualty became known or the day when the time – limit of article 281 (c) or of article 282 has been completed'. The time – limit of article 281 (c) is three or five months and of article 282 three months[271].

The three months time – limit starts running on the next day of the day when the casualty became known by certain information[272]. It is not necessary that specifically the assured knows the news. It is suffice that the news about the casualty was spread in the place where the assured lives[273]. If the assured had notified his declaration of abandonment before the time – limit commenced, the notified declaration is *invalid* because the right to abandonment has been exercised t o o e a r l y[274].

The right of the assured to notify his declaration of abandonment within a time – limit of three months operates in favour of the assured. The new law unified the different time – limits under the former law. It is argued that this new provision is a right choice of the legislator[275].

Article 288 of the Code (KINΔ) states: 'The underwriter has the right to set for the assured a specific and reasonable time – limit within which the assured may notify his declaration of abandonment. If such time – limit passes, the assured is deprived of the right to abandonment'. By introducing this provision the Hellenic Legislator attempts to strike a balance between the interests of the assured (article 283) and those of the insurer (article 288). In practice, however, this provision is not extensively used[276].

---

269 (82), p. 265. He is Thessaloniki legal author and tries to combine the two opposite views.

270 Although article 284 is not clear, declaration shall be unconditional. Balis (p. 257) argues that this is a reasonable requirement for the protection of the insurers' interests. Sarlis, p. 173; Skouloudis, p. 403.

271 N. 26 and n. 38.

272 Until the information is certain, the time – limit does not commence.

273 Sarlis, p. 172. Kiantos (p. 274) supports the view that the news has to be known to the assured himself. If the news is widely spread, the assured cannot invoke ignorance (like in the case of Titanic).

274 Kiantos (82), p. 278.

275 Sarlis, p. 171.

276 Argyriadis, p. 125.

‘Reasonable’ depends on the circumstances. It may be longer than three months, can be ten days but not four days. After the passing of the reasonable time – limit the right to abandonment is terminated[277].

ff. Acceptance of notice of abandonment

Article 285 of the Code (KINΔ) provides as follows: ‘If the insurer, within thirty days after the notification of the declaration of abandonment, does not raise doubts for the right to abandonment or if the right to abandonment is judicially acknowledged (recognised), the rights upon the remaining objects are transferred to the insurer. The transfer of the ownership is considered to have occurred immediately after the notification of the declaration of abandonment’.

In Hellenic law there is a limited right of the insurer to refuse to ‘accept’ the notified declaration of abandonment. He may declare (written or orally) to the assured, for example, that one of the cases of article 281 did not occur. Or he may refuse to indemnify the assured because the assured does not have the right to abandonment and the consequent right to indemnity. The mere silence of the insurer (*if he does not ‘refuse to accept’*) amounts to an acceptance in the sense that the insurer becomes the new owner of the remains. Therefore, he must indemnify the assured for a total loss. If the insurer wishes to decline ownership of the remains, he must also indemnify the assured for a total loss as article 287 of the Code (KINΔ) states. ‘The insurer may, by declaration notified to the assured immediately (after the notified declaration of abandonment), reject his right to ownership upon the abandoned subject – matter, indemnifying unconditionally the assured for a total loss’. It seems that the (financial) interests of the assured are well protected under the two provisions.

If there is mistake of fact after the insurer has indemnified the assured, the ‘acceptance’ of abandonment is irrevocable. The insurer may be the new owner of the ship which was not lost, and the assured may keep the indemnity. Of course, abandonment is revocable, if the two parties agree[278].

gg. The effect of abandonment

The effect of abandonment is that the insurer has all the rights upon the remains of the abandoned subject – matter insured the reason being that the assured is not allowed to become richer after being indemnified[279]. Transfer occurs thirty days after the notification of the declaration of abandonment to the underwriter (*unless he raised doubts over the right to abandonment)* (article 285). This has a retroactive effect and law settles the presumption that the transfer of all rights occurs immediately after the notification of the declaration (article 285). In other words, the insurer has such rights immediately after the notifica-

[277] Athens Court of First Instance (ΠΠΑθ) 6988 /1971, 39 (1972) EEN 87. Also, Kiantos, pp. 281 – 282.

[278] Kiantos, p. 285.

[279] Skouloudis, p. 400.

tion subject to the condition subsequent[280] that within thirty days after notification he may express doubts whether the right to abandonment legally arose.

In practice, the underwriters almost always raise doubts for the validity of the right to abandonment in order that they avoid take over the liabilities which accompany all rights upon the remains (for instance, wreck removal expenses)[281].

Alternatively, the insurer may follow the route settled in article 287. He may indemnify the assured for a total loss and decline his right to ownership on the remains. The right to ownership is legally equal to 'all rights'. This different term is not legally significant in the context of the discussed issues. It is argued[282] that the option under article 287 is better than the one under article 285 for the underwriter. In the latter case, it would probably cause more problems to the insurer because a trial is then inevitable and this means a continuing state of uncertainty for his interests (trials take a long time). Besides, he could lose on grounds that his 'refusal' did not fulfill the conditions under article 285. It is further argued that a more correct legislative solution is the English one, namely section 63(1) of the Act, in which abandonment gives to the insurer only a right to get the rights upon the remains[283]. On the contrary, in Hellenic law the insurer becomes the owner of the remains by law (article 285) and he may then discharge such liability. Once again, it seems that the interests of the assured are protected better than the interests of the underwriter. The balance is in favour of the underwriter under article 285(2). 'The assured is obliged to submit to the underwriter all the existing information and the documentary evidence'. However, the violation of article 285(2) rarely amounts to invalidity of abandonment. It is a secondary obligation in comparison to the effect of abandonment to the property of the underwriter.

Finally, if the insurer exercises his right under article 287, the rights on the remains belong to the assured[284]. But if the insurer exercises his right under article 285, two different opinions have been expressed. Either the rights on the remains belong to the assured until a final judgment is issued by the court[285]. Or the exercise of the rights of the insurer does not suspend the results of the abandonment[286]. Therefore, if the court decides that abandonment is lawful, the transfer is considered to have occurred (and have occurred) immediately after the notification of declaration of abandonment (article 285(1)). In the opposite case, the transfer is considered as not have occurred (and the assured is then responsible for the remains of the abandoned subject – matter insured).

---

[280] A condition subsequent is a provision that does not form part of a contractual (here, legal) obligation but operates to bring it to an end in certain specified circumstances (here, doubts). Martin, p. 94.

[281] Argyriadis, p. 125.

[282] Skouloudis, p. 404.

[283] Argyriadis, p. 126.

[284] Sarlis (p. 177) states that this is self – explanatory.

[285] Kiantos, p. 324.

[286] Kiantou – Pampouki, p. 82. Also, Spiliopoulos, p. 251, n. 8.

This is the correct view because it stays within the wording of article 285(1). Also, another strong legal argument relates to the legal nature of the judgment which 'recognises' the rights of the insurer on the remains (article 285(1)). Such type of judgment in Hellenic law has a specific legal dimension. It means that the court recognises a legal status. The status in the discussed case is that the remains belong to the insurer immediately after the notice of abandonment (notification of declaration of abandonment).

c. Comparison

The two legal systems appear to be similar in many aspects in relevance to notice of abandonment (although different terms are used: notification of declaration). First, notice of abandonment is the mean by which the assured exercises his right to abandon. If the assured fails to do so, the loss can only be treated in both legal orders as a partial loss. Second, the reason behind the requirement of notice of abandonment is also identically (underwriters may take steps to protect their interests). Also, the reason why the underwriters are entitled (or assumed by Hellenic law) to take over proprietary rights upon the remains of the abandoned subject – matter insured is the same. Unjust enrichment of the assured is forbidden in both the United Kingdom and the Hellenic marine insurance. Third, the questions who may give notice of abandonment and to whom it must be given are issues that the two statutes (the Act and the Code (ΚΙΝΔ)) deal with in the same way. Despite the fact that an agent of the insurer m a y be given notice, it is commonly accepted that the agent is n o t entitled to receive notice of abandonment. Fourth, notice of abandonment may be implied and m u s t be unconditional. This is an example where the United Kingdom and the Hellenic law arrives to the same legal principle after following different routes.

Even if there are similarities between the two legal orders, it is far too obvious that there are substantial differences between the English and the Hellenic marine insurance law regarding abandonment. First, the English Act specifies that 'notice of abandonment may be given in writing, or by word of mouth, or partly in writing and partly by word of mouth' (section 62(2)). On the other hand, article 284 of the Hellenic Code (ΚΙΝΔ) simply states that 'the right to abandonment is exercised by declaration notified to the underwriter'. This wording of the Hellenic provision leaves margin for opposite interpretations. As we have already seen, there is the view expressed by the Athenian Court and authors who argue that the notice of abandonment shall be in a written form. The authors from Thessaloniki support the opposite view (since the article does not specify, then the form may be written or oral). They also rely on section 62(2) of the Act. And there is the view of one other author from Thessaloniki which combines the two ones by stating that his city mates are right, but it is desirable that notice is given in written form. The fact is that in the United Kingdom this is a solved legal issue, whereas in Hellas there is a dispute over it the parties of which seems to belong to different cities (schools of law) and different way of legal thinking, albeit someone could argue that this may possibly be just a coincidence.

A second striking difference between the two legal systems relates to the time when the assured should give notice of abandonment to the underwriters. Here we observe a completely different function of the two systems. In English law, the assured must give notice of abandonment immediately after the receipt of reliable information (reasonable diligence) or within a reasonable time where the information is not perfectly clear (section 62(3) of the Act). Five days were held to have been unreasonable (*Hunt*). In Hellenic law, the assured may give notice of abandonment (notify the declaration of abandonment, in accurate Hellenic legal terms) within three months after the receipt of information of the loss (no distinction between reliable and uncertain information is made in the wording of provisions, so it is only for reliable information) (article 283 of the Code (ΚΙΝΔ)). Under article 288 the insurer may set a time – limit to the assured to give notice of abandonment but two days or one week is not within the requirement 'reasonable'. This difference between the two legal orders best illustrates what the legal term 'reasonable' means in different legal worlds. It is also accepted that in Hellenic law the interests of the assured are well protected.

Third, one other difference between the English Act and the Hellenic Code (ΚΙΝΔ) relates to acceptance of notice of abandonment by the underwriter. The underwriter under English law may accept or refuse to accept notice of abandonment (section 62(4), (5), (6) of the Act). This enables the insurer to wait to ascertain what the circumstances really are before he decides either to pay a total loss or to reject the abandonment. Mere silence is not an acceptance. And acceptance is a nullity, if it was based on fundamental mistake of fact. On the contrary, the underwriter under Hellenic law has only a limited right to accept notice. This is in favour of the assured. Mere silence of the insurer after notice means that he must indemnify the assured for a total loss and that he takes over the rights on the remains of the abandoned subject – matter insured. And if there is fundamental mistake of fact, notice and (possible) acceptance of abandonment is irrevocable unless the two parties agree the opposite. For one more time we see that in Hellenic law the interests of the assured are well protected.

Finally, there is one more striking difference between the United Kingdom and the Hellenic law. It regards the effect of abandonment. The underwriter takes over (article 285(1)) or is entitled to take over (section 63(1)) the interest of the assured in whatever may remain of the subject – matter insured, and all proprietary rights incidental thereto. The difference is twofold. First of all, the English law settles a simple system by stating that the insurer is entitled to take over the rights on the remains of the abandoned subject – matter insured. On the contrary, the Hellenic law settles the presumption that the transfer of property (of the subject – matter insured) occurs immediately and automatically (except the underwriter express doubts) after the notification of the declaration of abandonment (given notice of abandonment). Such transfer is subject to a condition subsequent: if in thirty days after the notification of the declaration of abandonment the insurer is not opposed to the legality of the r i g h t of abandonment, the transferred rights are finally belong to the insurer (article 285(1)). In practice, the underwriters choose to pay the total loss and decline rights on the remains of the abandoned subject – matter insured (article 287) to avoid the court proceedings. Then, the question is who the owner is.

The answer to the question relates to the second part of the discussed difference stems from the first part of it that we have just explained. In the United Kingdom, different views have been expressed. For example, it has been said that the insured ship, cargo or freight becomes *res nullius* if the underwriter declines to take over the rights on its remains. Later, the view changed, and the law is that in such case the assured remains the owner of the remains of the abandoned subject – matter insured. In Hellas, the answer depends on which article the insurer may rely to decline the rights on the remains. If it is article 287, the assured remains the owner of the remains. If the insurer invokes article 285, there is the view that the assured remains the owner of the remains. However, the presumption of article 285 shows the opposite direction: the insurer is the owner until the final judgment of the court.

If the assured remains owner and is indemnified for total loss, it seems that the principle of forbidden unjust enrichment does not apply. In practice, the underwriters avoid the wreck removal or other expenses that the assured pays in consequence. But in marine insurance law it seems that there is a problem. We state that the insurer takes over the remains because of the principle of forbidden unjust enrichment, and then we accept that the assured becomes the owner of the remains, if the underwriter does not want them. Practice affects law, but what if the insurer wants to avoid taking over the remains which have some real value? In the last Chapter of this Part we present a statutory model to propose possible solutions not only to the last question but also to the problems that we have discussed so far.

D. A statutory model

This statute would best operate if it would be adopted by all the European maritime nations (including the Hellenic Republic and the United Kingdom) in a possible European Union Regulation. Otherwise, it may be a sample for a hypothetical Hellenic or United Kingdom Act or part of the existing Code or Act.

*

Article 1
Scope of the statute

This Statute regulates the right to and notice of abandonment in marine insurance.

Article 2
Right to abandonment

The insured may abandon to the insurer the subject – matter insured and claim for a total loss in the cases and under the conditions of the following articles. The right to abandonment cannot be waived in a contract of marine insurance.

Article 3
Abandonment of the vessel insured

The abandonment of the vessel insured to the insurer is permitted only if:
(a) the vessel is lost by a peril insured against and its recovery from the assured is impossible within one month (equal to thirty days);
(b) the vessel is damaged by a peril insured against and the cost of repairs would exceed the three – fourths of the insured value. If the insured value is, at the time of the casualty, half the real value of the vessel or less, the real value shall be taken into account;
(c) the vessel has disappeared for one month. The thirty first day it is assumed that the vessel was lost by a peril insured against.
If the vessel appears within one month after the payment of a total loss, the vessel belongs to the insurer, but it is permitted that the abandonment may be rendered invalid by a Court, if the insured provides sufficient grounds thereon;
(d) the vessel is captured or detained by a foreign power for two months, provided that the contract of insurance covers war risks. 'Foreign' relates to the flag of the vessel insured.

Article 4
Abandonment of the cargo insured

The abandonment of the cargo insured is permitted only if:

(a) the cargo is lost by a peril insured against and its recovery from the insured is impossible within one month;
(b) the cargo is damaged by a peril insured against and the cost of repairs and forwarding it to is destination would exceed its value on arrival;
(c) the vessel has disappeared for one month and there is no news for the cargo;
(d) the cargo is captured or detained by a foreign power for one month or for less, if it is for seasonal goods, provided that the contract of insurance covers war risks. 'Foreign' relates to the nationality of the owner of the cargo insured.

Article 5
Abandonment of the freight insured

The abandonment of the freight insured is permitted only if one of the cases under article 3 occurs.

Article 6
Notice of abandonment

The right to abandonment is exercised by the insured giving valid notice of abandonment to the insurer.

Article 7
Valid notice of abandonment

Notice of abandonment is valid, if it:
(a) is unconditional,
(b) is in writing, and
(c) includes the word 'notice', or 'abandon', or 'abandonment'.

Article 8
Time limit

Notice of abandonment must be given to the insurer within fifteen (15) days after the casualty has been known to the insured.

If the information is of a doubtful character, notice must be given to the insurer within one month after the information has reached the insured.
No other time limits are allowed by way of individual agreements.

Article 9
Irrevocability

Notice of abandonment is irrevocable, unless exceptional circumstances have arisen.
The insurer is entitled to decide whether such circumstances justify the revocability of notice of abandonment.
The insurer shall not abuse such right to ignore the exceptional circumstances, so he must give to the insured special reasoning in writing, if he denies accepting that such circumstances arose.

Article 10
Effect of abandonment

If the underwriter does not take over the proprietary rights to the remains of the abandoned subject – matter insured within one month after notice of abandonment was given to him, the rights remain in the ownership of the insured who has been indemnified for total loss.
This provision does not prejudice the insurance legal principle of the forbidden unjust enrichment of the insured.

*

The aforementioned statutory model combines the provisions of the United Kingdom Act 1906 and the Hellenic Code (KINΔ). It may solve the legal problems that we have discussed throughout the present Part of the text. Of course, many more legal issues could have been dealt with and the discussed legal issues may be analysed much further. The limited space in the present text gave us the opportunity to attempt to approach the Hellenic and the English law which sufficiently covers issues relating to collision liability but seems to cause difficulties in relevance to abandonment.

PART III
BURDEN AND STANDARD OF PROOF

In the above mentioned context of collision liability and abandonment, it is extremely important to clarify mainly in UK the burden and standard of proof in the litigation process.

Before a valid claim can be submitted under a marine insurance policy, it is necessary that a loss or damage shall have occurred from a peril insured against. Where the assured wishes to recover under his insurance, he must prove that the loss or damage falls within the covered risk. Not only is his obligation relating to the burden and standard of proof as it applies before the English courts of Common Law; it is also required in an earlier stage. The insurer avoids to pay an unproven claim; in the first place this is the main reason why he may find himself defending his interests before the court. The general rule in relation to the standard of proof in marine insurance cases is based on the rule which applies to any civil case: the balance of probabilities (as opposed to 'beyond reasonable doubt' which is the standard of proof applied in criminal cases).

The legal rule regarding burden of proof is well established: the plaintiff (who shall be in most cases the assured) must prove his case. Even then, he is expected to adduce sufficient evidence that he had an insurable interest at the time of the loss. Where the loss is unexplainable, the law settles the presumption that the loss has been caused by a peril insured against. In all other cases, the plaintiff must prove the proximate cause of the loss or whether the vessel (*his* vessel or the vessel) has been lost by a war risk or by a marine risk.

The main defence of the insurer (who shall be in most cases the defendant) is the wilful misconduct of the assured, or the excepted perils. The insurer may decide to pay an unproven claim, even if he is suspicious of the claimant. However, if he does not pay the assured and he is the defendant before the court, he bears the onus of proving (by producing evidence and by persuading) his allegation.

In practice, arbitration is a preferable way of dispute resolution, but the rules of burden and standard of proof also apply (directly or indirectly) to such proceedings. Of course, it is not always easy to identify the clarity of this rules, especially in the case of barratry.

A. The early stage: proof of loss before bringing an action

a. General

A ship with cargo on board sinks to the bottom of the sea. The ship owner, cargo owner, mortgagee, assignee or other interested parties[287] claim for the loss

[287] Hodges, p.245. The question 'who can sue a marine policy?' is answered in Arnould's, p.1132. I deal with it in the next paragraph.

under the marine insurance policy. The insurer can defend the claim simply and 'cheaply' by doing nothing[288].

In such cases, the assured must prove the truth of his claim[289]. It is common sense that the 'burden of proof' lies with the assured. This means that the insurer will not pay the claim, unless he is convinced that the assured is telling him the truth. However, suspicion of claimants seems to be a recognised occupational hazard[290]. I remember a movie with Danny De Vito (he was the insurer) where he did all he could to avoid paying the claim! This is the job of the insurer[291].

The standard of proof can be understood in the context of a civil action, but it is also required to satisfy the insurer. As I see it, if the insurer is not one hundred percent sure that the vessel was lost or damaged by a proximate cause of peril insured against and without any fraudulent intervention of the assured, he shall not be ready to pay the claim. Given the fact that it is much difficult for the assured to persuade the insurer 'beyond any reasonable doubt', it seems a much lower test for the assured the balance of probabilities[292] that the law requires in a civil case.

b. Insurable interest

The law requires not only that the assured has an insurable interest at the time of loss, but also, that he proves such interest existing at time of loss when submitting a claim to underwriter[293]. In cases of great difficulty for the assured in proving the extent of his insurable interest, the underwriter may be prepared to cover the assured, but to waive all rights to have insurable interest proved in the event of a claim. Such policy is void[294].

---

[288] Clark, pp. 165-166 indicates three other possibilities for the insurer to defend himself: firstly, for a more active defence before the court, the insurer has various moves to test the strength of the claim (Against a fire claim, for example, the insurer may subpoena documents relating to the claimant's financial affairs). Secondly, the insurer has time on his side. Unlike the United States (the insurer who is slow to pay is liable to pay punitive damages for 'bad faith') rules, there is little or no legal sanction against the slow insurer in England. Thirdly, the insurer's practice is to have claims investigated by their own claims inspectors or, if the claim is large or difficult, by loss adjusters.

[289] This may be based on a peril of the seas, fire, barratry or war risk. I pursue to identify the relevant legal issues in the next Chapter.

[290] Clarke, p.164.

[291] Stamelos, pp. 164-166.

[292] Hodges, (p.253) says that the legal requirement of proof on b or p is to be applied with common sense. She was advocate by the Law Lords in The Popi M (1985) 2 Lloyd's Rep. 1, HL.

[293] Brown (p. 160) states that under English law a Policy Proof of Interest Policy that waves proof of interest is void. Bennett, pp. 13-19.

[294] In the previous footnote this legal aspect is further explained.

B. Bringing the action before the court: the assured seeks to recover

a. Who is the plaintiff?

aa. The assured

It is not always possible to answer this question. What I can say for sure is that the plaintiff is the assured whenever he wishes to proceed against the liability insurer to ascertain or enforce recover from the insurer. This is the first procedural question arising in relation to liability insurance as it is stated in Arnould's[295]. Being seen in another way, it is discussed the matter of whether the assured is entitled to join the liability insurer as third party in an action brought against the assured by the claimant. I comment on this in the last Chapter of this text. The plaintiff is the insurer in the case of appealing a judgement on the successful action brought by the assured (the appellant insurer) or in the case of discovering that he paid the claim to the assured who casted away the vessel (or his vessel).

These are the most common possibilities. The plaintiff is the assured[296] in most actions. This can be proved 'beyond any reasonable doubt' if someone observed the cases commented by the authors on marine insurance relating to the burden and standard of proof[297].

bb. Whoever must prove his case

Irrespective of the plaintiff's identity (assured or insurer), it is worth answering the question (who is the plaintiff?) in another way. He is not the vulnerable or the strong party. Law does not protect him. The burden of proof lies with the plaintiff throughout the litigation[298] because 'marine insurance cases afford no exception to the general rule that...plaintiff...must prove his case'[299]. Besides, it would not be proper to search for principles of fair justice in this rule. Two equal

---

[295] P. 1132.

[296] As I have already said in the previous paragraph (footnote 1) in Arnould's, p. 1132 it is answered the question 'who can sue on a marine policy?'. An action on a policy can be brought in the name of a broker.

[297] Banco de Barcelona and Others v Union Marine Insurance Co Ltd (1925) 30 Cay Cas 316; Compania Naviera Royal Exchange Assurance Corp (1923) K.B. 650. Cobb & Jenkins v Volga Insurance Co Ltd of Petrograd (1920) 4 Ll L Rep 130; Michelos & Sons Maritime S.A v Prudential Assurance co. LTD.(The Zinovia) (1984) 2 Lloyd., Rep, 264.

[298] As Hodges p.247 mentions 'the burden of proof is and remains throughout on the plaintiffs' by referring to the Popi M, (1985) 2 Lloyd's Rep 264.

[299] In Banco de Barcelona Mr. Justice Greer at 317 goes on: 'that is to say, he must establish his cause of action to the reasonable satisfaction of the tribunal'. In addition, a person who claims a salvage reward has the burden of proving his entitlement to such a reward (in Kenedy, p.407).

parties are fighting for their interests before the court; whoever starts the fight, he is obliged to prove why he does it[300].

b. What exactly is the plaintiff required to prove?

aa. Insurable interest.

Section 6 (1) of Marine Insurance Act 1906 requires the assured to have an insurable interest in the subject-matter (the vessel or the cargo) insured at the time of the loss[301]. The onus is on the plaintiff of proving that his interest was intended to be insured under the policy[302].

On the other hand, section 4 (2) b of Marine Insurance Act 1906 declares a PPI policy as being 'void', which is the basis for rejection of these policies by the courts[303].Void does not mean illegal. However, the burden of proof lies with the assured who brings the action against the insurer. The assured must prove his insurable interest based upon the terms of the marine insurance contract. The slip is the evidence of the terms of the contract[304]. Section 89 of the Marine Insurance Act 1906 provides that 'reference may be made to the slip or covering note, in any legal proceeding'[305].

bb. War risk.

Whether a vessel has been lost by a war risk or by a marine risk is a matter of fact, and the burden of proof of loss lies on the assured[306]. He must produce suf-

---

300 In criminal cases, the law protects the vulnerable party, the man who is in charge, because the prosecutor, the state, is stronger than him. Androulakis (in p. 192) concludes that in the penal procedure there is not the concept. Justice Compania Naviera S.A. v Prudential Assurance Co. Ltd. (The Ilavian Reefer), (1995)

301 Bennett, pp. 13-19 explains the general rules on insurable interest.

302 Arnould's, p. 157, where three relevant cases are mentioned: Boston Fruit 6 v British and Foreign Mar. Ins. 6. [1905] 1 K.B. 637 (at p. 646); Vangtsze Ins. Ass. v Lukmanjee [1918] A. C. 585 (PC); Graham Joint Stock Shipping Co. V Merchants' Mar. Ins. Co. [1923] 1 K.B. 592 at p. 634.

303 Brown, p. 161.

304 Certain policies are issued on terms which require no further proof of interest than the document itself as Goodacre (p. 35) says

305 Brown, pp 42-43 deals with the slip as evidence. I also comment on this legal issue in the last chapter of this text.

306 Ivamy, pp. 207-209, refers to eleven relevant cases: General Steam Navigation Co Ltd. v Jonson (1915) 31 TLR 630, KBD; Euterpe SS Co Ltd v North of England Protecting and Indemnity Association Ltd (1917) 33 TLR 540, KBD; British and Burmese Steam Navigation Co Ltd v Liverpool and London War Risks Insurance Association Ltd, and British and Foreign Marine Insurance Co Ltd (1917) 34 TLR 140, KBD; Compania Maritima of Barcelona v Wishart (1918) 23 Com Cas 264; Munro Brice & Co v Fw Marten (1920) 2 Ll.L. Rep 25; Mitrovich Bros & Co v Merchants Marine Insurance Co. Ltd (1923) 14 Ll. L. Rep. 25; De Marco and Gazan v Scottish Metropolitan Assurance Co (1923) 14 Ll.L. Rep 173; Zachariassen v Importers' and Exporters' Marine Insurance Co. Ltd (1923) 18 Ll L Rep 98, CA; General

ficient evidence and persuade the court that the vessel was lost by a war risk. For example, in De Marco and Gazan v Scottish Metropolitan Assurance Co[307] a vessel was insured against war risks. After she had shunk whilst she was about twenty-two miles north of Cape Dukato, the assured claimed for a loss under the policy on the ground that she had been lost by a mine. Evidence was given as to the presence of mines in the neighbourhood. Roche J, held that the action failed because the assured had failed to prove that she had been lost by a war peril. In other words, the plaintiff or the assured failed to discharge the burden of proof which throughout lies on him.

In a steam trawler sailed from Aberdeen on 28 January 1942. She sank because of an underwater explosion. Atkinson J, held that the assured had discharged the burden of showing (by evidence and persuasion) that she had been holed as the result of contact with an explosive float, and that she had therefore been lost by a war risk.

cc. Peril of the sea.

Where peril of the sea is asserted as the proximate cause of loss, the assured must establish a prima[308] facie case of '...fortuitous accidents or casualties of the seas...'.

As a general rule, the plaintiff assured has to provide direct proof[309] pointing to a specific[310] accident or casualty responsible for the loss[311].

If the assured is unable to provide clear proof of a casualty or accident to demonstrate that the loss was caused by a peril of the sea, he has failed to prove his case. The burdens of proof is and remains throughout the litigation on the plaintiff assured[312].

Stem Navigation Co v R (1927) 27 Ll L Rep 366, KBD; United Scottish Insurance Co. Ltd v British Firhing Vessel Mutual War Risks Association Ltd: The Braconbush (1944) 78 Ll L Rep 70, KBD.

307 (1923) 14 Ll L Rep 173 at 220.

308 Marine Insurance Act 1906, Sched. 1, rule 7. Hazelwood in Thomas (p.145), Bennett (p.107) and Hodges (p.246) remind us the general rule regarding the burden of proof as it applies (like any other civil action) to marine insurance claims before a court of law.

309 This is related to the evidence which is analysed in the last Chapter of this text.

310 Refers to British & Foreign Marine Insurance Co. Ltd. v Gamt (1921) 2 A.C.-41, 57-58 and Bennett points out (in p. 109) that where insurance covers 'all risks' the assured' s burden is considerably eased. The precise cause may remain in doubt yet the assured will recover. Hodges in p. 219 also refers to 'all risks' issue.

311 Hodges, pp. 246-247 refers to 'the Tropaioforos' case (Compania Naviera Santi SA v Indemnity Marine Insurance co Ltd [1960] 2 Lloyd' s Rep 469 at p.473 and what Mr Justice Pearson remarked ('the plaintiffs have the burden of proving that there was an accidental loss by perils of the seas').

312 Hodges (p.247) establishes this rule on the case law: 'The Popi M' case (1985) 2 Lloyd's Rep 1, HL; Miceli v Union Marine & General Insurance Co Ltd (1938), Co Ll.L Rep. 275.

To discharge the burden of proof the assured must produce sufficient evidence to satisfy the court that the subject-matter insured (vessel or cargo) was lost by a peril of the sea.

It is a completely different legal issue what constitutes 'clear proof' and what is the sufficient degree of proof that the court requires in order to be satisfied.

What is actually important here can be summarized by the phrase that: if the assured brings an action against the insurer based upon the peril of the sea claim, the plaintiff assured bears the burden of proving that a specific peril of the sea caused the loss of the vessel (or his vessel) or the cargo insured.

dd. Fire.

If the plaintiff assured claims for a loss caused by fire, he has the burden of proving his claim. It is not difficult, however, for the assured to prove it. He can easily discharge the onus of proof because he is not required to prove the fortuity of the fire. He must only prove that the fire occurred and, therefore, the loss occurred.

If someone compares the burden of proving a peril of the sea which lies with the plaintiff to the onus of proving fire which also lies with the plaintiff, he could conclude that a plaintiff who claims upon fire is luckier[313] than the other plaintiff. Indeed, peril of the sea refers only to fortuitous accidents or casualties of the sea by the legal definition which can be fund in Schedule 1 rule 7 of the Marine Insurance Act 1906 (and this definition has been developed by the courts[314]).

When fire is the proximate case of the loss other issues are of importance: for example, whether 'mere heating' or 'flames' are (which actually are not) within the specific meaning of 'fire'[315].

If the plaintiff assured proves the fire as the proximate cause of the loss, he shall discharge the onus of proof.

In this case the legal rule relating to the civil procedure operates in favour of the plaintiff because of the substantive legal definition of fire. It is not a choice made by the legislator; it is a legal consequence of both rules. I mention it to emphasize once again that the burden of proof regulation is not relevant to principles of fair justice, but relating to common sense[316].

---

313 Hodges (in p.271) uses the expression: lesser burden of proof. Slattery v Mance [(1962)1 All Er 525 at p.526] is the authority which has established the rule that 'once it is shown that the loss has been caused by fire, the plaintiff has made out a *prima facie* case'.

314 Bennett (in pp.137-139) mentions the relevant cases, for example, Magnus v Buttemer (1924) A.C. 431.

315 Bennett p.148. Tempus Shipping Co Ltd v Dreyfus & Co Ltd (1930) 1 K.B. 699 is a typical case which dealt with such matters.

316 I have already made this point clear in the paragraph *Who is the plaintiff?*

ee. Barratry.

Barratry of master officers or crew is defined in rule 11 of the Rules of Construction in the Marine Insurance Act 1906, and is said to include: '...every wrongful act wilfully committed by the master or crew to the prejudice of the owner, or, as the case may be, the charterer'[317].

The 6.2 clause of the Institute Time Clauses Hulls (the 4.2 clause of the Institute Voyage Clauses Freight and the 4.2 clause of the Institute Voyage Clauses Freight) provides that: 'this insurance covers loss of the subject-matter insured caused by [6.2.4] barratry...'[318].

The most obvious 'wrongful act' would be sending the vessel to the bottom[319].

The peril of 'barratry' is two things: first, a deliberate wrongdoing (for example, sinking the vessel) by a member of the crew; plus, prejudice to the owner (i.e. without his privity).

According to the general principles of marine insurance litigation, the assured must establish a *prima facie* case by offering evidence of both elements to the definition of the peril.

In other words, he must prove that: (a) Members of the crew caused the loss of the vessel (or his vessel)[320]; (b) this was made to his prejudice. This means 'without his consent or...without his privity'[321].

Two provisions are crucial to the discussed legal matter: (1) section 55 (2)a of the Marine Insurance Act 1906 which provides that the insurer is liable for any loss..., even though the loss would not have happened but for the misconduct or negligence of the master or crew. (2)The subparagraph within the 6.2 clause of the Institute Time Clauses Hulls provides that: '...provided that such loss has not resulted from want of due diligence by the assured, owners, managers or superintendents or any of their onshore management'.

The legal value of section 55(2)a can be best described as follows: the legislator permits the assured to recover, even if a man's action caused the loss of the vessel (or cargo).

On the contrary, the assured cannot recover under the marine insurance policy, if the man's action caused the loss has been controlled by him, the assured.

---

317 Hazelwood in Thomas, pp.156-157.

318 Bennett, in p.155 argues that this clause (referred to the 'Inchmaree clause') is of somewhat broader scope.

319 Hazelwood in Thomas, p.157

320 This may be a barratrous fire.

321 The interpretation of the phraze 'to the prejudice of the owner' has been made in Piermay Shipping co. SA and Brandt's Ltd v Chester (The Michael) (1979) 1 Lloyd's Rep. 55 at p.66, per Kerr J. Definitions are also provided in: Compania Naviera Martiartu v REA Corpn. (1924) 19 Ll L Rep 95 at 96, per Lord Birkenhead; Elfie A Issaias v Marine Insurance Co. Ltd. (1923) 15 Ll L Rep 186 at 191, 192, per Atkin LJ, and at 189, per Warrington LJ.

This condition is settled in the subparagraph within the 6.2 clause of the Institute Time Clauses Hulls[322]. The law requires 'something more' from the assured, if he wishes to claim for the loss of the subject-matter insured.

Therefore, the assured bears the burden of proof which is twofold: first, he must prove the misconduct of the master or crew[323]; secondly, he must prove that he was not involved in such misconduct. This is also said to be the twin burden of proof[324] in the 'the Michael' case[325], in 'the Spathari' case[326].

On the other hand, a series of cases[327] introduces the opposite rule: the defendant (insurer) must prove that the assured did consent to the misconduct of the crew. This has caused legal problems which are discussed in the last Chapter of this text.

To summarize the paragraph, it has to be said that the burden of proof is on the assured to produce evidence and satisfy the court that the vessel was scuttled without his privity. If he fails to prove it, he shall not be entitled to recover.

ff. Seaworthiness.

Although the onus of proof of seaworthiness is on the insurers[328], there is one class of case in which the insured will find it necessary to establish seaworthiness in order to prove his case. This is where the insured, having no direct evidence of loss due to a fortuitous event, seeks to establish by inference a case of loss due to an unascertained peril of the sea. To justify the inference he will seek to exclude the possibility of loss caused by unseaworthiness by calling evidence as to the condition of the ship.

gg. Total loss

In policies warranted free of particular average[329], the burden of proving a total loss lies on the assured. Despite the fact that the burden of proof falls upon the insurer (where the cover is subject to specific exclusion[330]), a reverse burden clause may oblige the assured to disprove the operation of an exclusion (where the insurer presents an arguable case for the operation of an exclusion and satis-

[322] It is never necessary for the assured to prove that the master was not the owner: Ross v Hunter (1790) 4 Term Rep 33, in Ivamy, p.169

[323] Hodges, (in p.263) points out that the Court of Appeal in 'the Martiartu' case (1923) 1 KB 650, CA [which was affirmed by the House of Lords (1924) 19 Ll L Rep 95], in the context of barratry, did not make it explicitly clear which party has to prove the issue of consent.

[324] Hodges, (in p.263) points out that the Court of Appeal in 'the Martiartu' case (1923) 1 KB 650, CA [which was affirmed by the House of Lords (1924) 19 Ll L Rep 95], in the context of barratry, did not make it explicitly clear which party has to prove the issue of consent.

[325] (1979) 1 Lloyd's Rep 55; (1979) 2 Lloyd's Rep. 1 CA.

[326] (1924) 21 Ll L Rep 265.

[327] Issaias and other cases mentioned in Chapter D.

[328] I discuss it in the next Chapter.

[329] Bennett, p.110.

[330] Green v Brown (1744)2 Str. 1 199.

faction of the casual connection required by the policy between the exclusion and the loss).

c. Which is the required standard of proof?

aa. The presumption of loss by 'peril of the sea' in unexplainable losses

Section 58 of the Marine Insurance Act 1906 provides that where the vessel is missing after the lapse of a 'reasonable time' and there is no news of her, an actual total loss 'may be presumed'. However, it remains necessary for the assured to prove that the loss proximately caused by a peril insured against.

If the vessel sank, and no evidence is left, no one can prove the proximate cause of the loss.

The assured must prove that the vessel was seaworthy on a balance of probabilities. Then, the presumption operates in the way that the vessel sank because of a peril of the sea insured against.

In other words, the required standard of proof amounts to the presumption of loss by 'peril of the sea' (technically inaccurate: the loss could have arisen from other events) and this has nothing to do with the balance of probabilities[331]. It is the lowest standard of proof required (reminds us the 'all risk' rule because it is 'rebuttable' as the burden then shifts to underwriters to prove an exception to liability) and it is different from the standard of proof required in all other cases.

bb. The balance of probability in all other cases

The degree or standard of proof required to satisfy the court is not always the same; however, the general rule (applicable to all civil actions) is that the plaintiff has to prove on a balance of probabilities that the ship was lost by a peril of the sea[332], by fire, by barratry or by war risk. The judge must, on the evidence, be satisfied that the event, as alleged, is more likely to have occurred than not[333].

---

[331] An explanation as to nature of the presumption was attempted by Dillon LJ in *The Marel*, where he explained that in his view the presumption was founded on the balance of probabilities: His Lordship said that if it is known that the ship is seaworthy when she sets out and is not seen since and nothing is heard of her crew, then, Dillon LJ suggested:

'...she must have sunk and, on the balance of probabilities, the sinking must have been due to "perils of the sea" because she was seaworthy when she set out. The only alternative would be that she was scuttled, but members of the ship's company who scuttle their ship do not normally intend to commit suicide. They expect to be rescued'.

This explanation cannot be correct. It is based upon the premise that once unseaworthiness is excluded there can be no other cause of the loss and that the „only alternative" would be a loss by perils of the seas.

[332] Even if unexplained. Useful comments on this legal issue are made by Hazelwood in Thomas, p. 155.

[333] Hodges (in p.253) refers to 'the Popi M' case (1985) 2 Lloyd's Rep 1, HL and to 'the Tropaioforos' case (1960) 2 Lloyd's Rep 469 at p.473.

Bennett (in p.109) refers to Kerr v Ayr Steams Shipping Co. Ltd. (1915) A.C. 217, to Compania Maritima of Barcelona v Wishart (1918) 23 Cons Cas 264, to United Scottish Insurance

C. Defence against the action: the insurer seeks to avoid paying the claim

a. Who is the defendant?

It is suffice to say that the same observations apply here mutatis mutandis as already mentioned in the paragraph a) of the previous Chapter.

b. What exactly is the defendant required to prove? (or) what are the means of his defence?

aa. Unseaworthiness

One of the three[334] implied warranties set out in Marine Insurance Act 1906 is a warranty of seaworthiness of the ship. Section 39(4) of the Act states: 'A ship is deemed to be seaworthy...'[335].

The burden of proving a breach of warranty lies upon the under-writer[336].Therefore, the burden of proving a breach of the implied warranty of seaworthiness lies on the insurer where he alleges it[337].

He is making the allegation that the ship is unseaworthy and it is natural that he should bear the onus of proof[338].

Additionally, there is no presumption of law[339] that a ship is unseaworthy because she breaks down or sinks from an unexplained cause (not unexplainable

---

Co. Ltd. V British Fishing Vessels Mutual War Risks Association Ltd (The Braconbush) (1945)78 Ll L Rep 70. O' May in pp.158, 322-323 refers to the same rule.

334 Hodges (in p.135) helpfully adds that English law does not impose a warranty of seaworth on a time policy by mentioning Gibson v Small (1853)4 HL Cas 353 (in p.250) the 'Marel'case (1992) 1 Lloyd Rep 420 and section 39 (5) of the Marine Insurance Act 1906. Ivamy (in p.297) refers to the two other implied warranties as they are settled down in section 40(2) and 41 of the Marine Insurance Act 1906: ship reasonably fit to carry the goods to the destination and the adventure insured is a lawful one.

335 Hodges (in p.134) says that Parker v Potts (1815) 3 Dow 23 is the authority which has enunciated the general rule that 'a ship is *prima facie* to be deemed seaworthy'.

336 In Arnold's (in p.528), it is said that 'this even where compliance is expressed to be a condition precedent to recovery under the policy. Colinvaux (in p.114) also refers to the case which settles the rule stated in the text: Band Air Services Ltd v Hill (1955). He also refers to an older case: Stebbing v Liverpool & London & Globe (1917) 2 K.B. 433, 438.

337 Ivamy (in p.298) makes reference to three cases: Parker v Pottis (1815) 3 Dow 23; Franco von Natusch (1836) Tyr & Gr 401; Pickum v Thames and Mersey Marine Insurance Co (1878) 3 QBD 594, CA. In Arnould's (in p.579) it is also mentioned the case: Davidson v Burnard (1868) L.R. 4 C.P. 117. Bennett (in p.300) refers to: C. Hoffmann & Co. v British General Insurance co. (1922) 10 Ll L Rep434.

338 Hodges (in p.134) highlights that this is in accordance with the general principle of the law of evidence: he who alleges must prove.

339 Carver (in p.124) refers to Ajvns Goolacy v Union Marine Insurance (1901) A.C. 362 and to Commercial Molasses v New York Tank; Barge Co. (1941) 314 U.S. 104. In Arnould's (in p.579) reference is made to Pickup v Thames Ins. Co. (1878) 3 Q.B.D. 594 and to other US cases.

cause). However, such facts may in some circumstances raise an inference, or presumption of fact, of unseaworthiness. Thus, the burden of proof is shifted on to the assured.

bb. Denying.

It is always for the plaintiff (assured) to prove a *prima facie* loss by a peril insured against. In theory[340], it remains open to the defendant (insurer) to rest his defence on ground that the assured has failed to prove loss by an insured peril.

In the case of Regina Fur Co Ltd v Bossay[341] all the judges were agreed that in so far as the underwriters merely denied that the loss was caused by the alleged peril insured against and put the assured to his proof, then the burden remained on the assured[342].

It is worth saying here that in practice[343] the insurer would follow one of the other means of defence (as they analyzed below), because he would try at least to cause doubts to the judges about the truth of the plaintiff's claims: In order for the defendant to achieve this aim, he would try to do something more than simply denying what the plaintiff tries to prove.

cc. Excepted peril

The burden of proving that a loss falls within an excepted peril always falls upon the insurer[344]. It is for him to show that the peril is not covered or is excluded[345]. Issues such as ordinary wear and tear and inherent vice[346] are raised by the insurer; the onus of proof rests upon the insurer[347].

The District Court for the Eastern District of Virginia, Norfolk Division held that the presumption that she was unseaworthy had not been satisfactorily rebutted by the assured. Ivamy (in p. 298) points out Capital Coastal Shipping Corpn and Bulk Tawing Corpn v Hartfordfire Insurance Co. (United States of America, Third Party: The Christie (1975) 2 Lloyd's Rep. 100

[340] In Arnould's, p.580, this means of defence is examined in the context of the defence of unseaworthiness that the insurer may follow.

[341] (1958) 2 Lloyd's Rep. 425. The assured must prove a loss due to a risk insured against.

[342] Hazelwood (in p.165) discusses the matter in relation to the positive defence of casting away the vessel with privity that the underwriter may establish.

[343] Practice in courts is sometimes different from theory regarding rules which regulate civil procedure aspects. This matter is briefly commented in the last Chapter of this text.

[344] Colinvaux, p.338

[345] Schmitthoff (in p.527) refers to M. Golodetz and Co. Inc. V Garnikow-Rionda Co.Inc. [1980] 1 W.L.R.495 at 513.

[346] Goodacre, p.34.

[347] Bennett (in p.138) also states that in the context of peril of the sea-fortuity being part of the definition of the peril reverses this burden-requires the assured to show that the loss was not attributable to such causes.

In the Popi M[348] case the vessel sank due to unexplained entry of sea water into her engine room trough a hole in the shell plating. This occurred off Algeria in good weather and sea conditions.

Bingham J, at first instance, felt unable to accept underwriters' defence based on expert evidence of wear and tear[349]. So, inherently improbable as it was, he accepted the assured's theory of collision with a submarine.

Lord Brandon in the House of Lords suggested that the judge's view was based on Sherlock Holmes' dictum to Dr. Watson: 'When you have eliminated the impossible, whatever remains, however improbable must be the truth'.

The Court should, he said, have followed Sevutton L.J. in La Compania Naviera Martiartu v Royal Exchange[350] and, where the evidence left him in doubt as to the course of the aperture in the ship's with the assured had failed to discharge the burden of proof upon them, and the claim failed.

dd. Mispresentation

Mispresentation is usually set up by the insurer as a defence to an action on the policy, and on him therefore will rest the burden of proof, and the mispresentation relied on must be established very clearly[351].

---

348 Rhesa Shipping Co.SA v Edmunds (The Popi M) (1985)2 Lloyd's Rep 1; (1985)1 W.L.R. 948; (1985)2 All E.R. 712. For another example O' May refers to Lamb Head Shipping Co Ltd v Jennings (The Marel) (1992)1 Lloyd's Rep. 402.

349 O' May (in p.323) discusses the defence of the underwriters in the context of the unexplained loss that occurred in the Popi M case.

350 La Compania Martiartu v The Cooperation of the Royal Exchange Assurance (1923) 1 K.B. 650 at 657; (1922) 13 Ll.L.Rep. 298 at 304. Unexplained losses are different from unexplainable losses as it has already been explained in this text (this distinction is made by Hazelnut, in p.156).

351 Ivamy (in p.78) is based on Davies v National Fire and Marine Insurance Co. of New Zealand (1891) AC 485 and Elkin v Janson (1845)13 M&W 655. I would like to add at this point that breach of good faith by the assured could also be a defence by the insurer. Thus, the insurer shall bear the onus of proof in such case. Material mispresentation (breach of good faith [for an in-depth analysis of good faith see also Botes, Peter Lang, 2006]) is the defence of the insurer against the assured as Brown (in p.158) explains. The underwriter must prove this allegation; otherwise, the court will not accept it and the allegation of the insurer shall fail. To the 'effective defence' (breach of good faith) reference is also made by Goodacre in p.34. He also points out that the onus of proving the defence lies on the underwriters (party pleading it), and this duty can be extremely onerous. Beale, Bishop, Furmston (in pp.321-349) and McKendrick (in pp. 234-254) analyse mispresentation in the context of contract law. Fraudulent mispresentation (in contract law) differs from fraud (in Criminal law) as it is explained by Spyridakis, in p.611. It is stated that the German Civil Code says '*arglistige Täuschung*' [civil law fraudulent mispresentation] instead of '*Betrug*' which is used in the German Penal Code. "Arglistig" means fraudulent, see Bugg, p. 419. "Täuschung" means mispresentation, see Bugg, p. 561. Article 318(2) of the German Civil Code (Bürgerliches Gesetzbuch, BGB) provides that "*Die Anfechtung der getroffenen Bestimmung wegen Irrtums, Drohung oder arglistiger Täuschung steht nur den Vertragschliessenden zu*". For the text of the article see Köhler, p. 71. For the theoretic analysis of the article see Medicus, pp. 126, 206, 417, 528,

ee. Wilful Misconduct

'Ships are not cast away out of lightness of heart or sheer animal spirits...there must be a hope of gain, and that is the owner's'[352]. Wilful misconduct means[353] 'intentionally doing something that is wrong'. For the purposes of this analysis, the assured intentionally casts away his vessel. Casting away is something wrong, because it goes against the fundamental principle of marine insurance: 'no man may take advantage of his own wrong'[354]. In consequence, the underwriter is not liable[355]. Section 55(2)a of the Marine Insurance Act 1906 provides for the non-liability of the insurer if the loss was attributable to the wilful misconduct of the assured. It is obvious that the insurer's main defence would be to prove that the assured intentionally caused the loss in order to recover. This defence is dealt separately, although wilful misconduct is an excepted peril, because of its great legal value and importance. It must be said that the insurer may bring this allegation to defend himself in claims of the assured based either on peril of the sea, and barratry, or on fire.

Fire

If the insurer wishes to prove that the fire was deliberately caused by the assured, the onus of proof lies on the insurer[356]. If he fails to prove that the assured involved in starting the fire to recover because of the loss, the assured will be entitled to recover.

---

531. For the systematic analysis of the article see Palandt, p. 516. Article 263 of the German Penal Code (Strafgesetzbuch) is titled "*Betrug*" meaning "Criminal Fraud". For the text of the article see Weigend, p. 123. For the analysis of the article see Tröndle, pp. 1735-1796. For the analysis of the notion in the context of the European Community [article 280 of the EC Treaty, the German title is: "*Bekämpfung von Betrug zum Nachteil der EG*", see Classen, p. 138; ex-article 209A has been amended by article Z.77 TEU and article 2.52 Amsterdam Treaty, see Scandamis, p. 179. For the English text of ex-article 209A see Foster, p. 90], see Satzger, p. 89. In Hellas, the term "fraud" is used in both codes, civil and criminal, having different meanings. Burden of proof in Hellenic maritime law is discussed by Skantzakis in pp. 324, 413, 431: branches of insurance.

[352] Compania Naviera Martiartu v Royal Exchange Assurance Corpn. (The Arnus) (1924) 19 Ll.L.Rep.95 at 99, Lord Summer.

[353] Martin, p.501.

[354] Ivamy (in p.232) reminds us that this principle is applied in all branches of insurance.

[355] The underwriter is not liable in case it is proven that wilful misconduct was either the proximate cause or a remote cause of the loss. This is due to the interpretation of the wording of section 55(2)a of the Marine Insurance Act 1906 ('attributable to') that Mr. Wight suggested in his Lecture, 12 /3 /99, University of Essex.

[356] Colinvaux (in p.90) refers to Bater v Bater [1951] p.35, 36,37 and to Stattery v Mance (1962) 1 Q.B.676. Ivamy (in p.238) refers to Empire SS Co Ins v Threadneedle Insurance Co (1925) 22 Ll L Rep 437, 534.

Barratry

If the insurer wishes to content that barratry happened with the connivance of the assured, he is not required to prove it. He does not bear the onus of proof. However there are cases which settle the rule that the insurer must prove that barratry occurred without the consent of the plaintiff assured. Issaias is the case which introduced this rule and there are other cases which either followed the rule or did not follow it, but took it into consideration. This contradiction is not intended to be discussed here but in the next Chapter. It is enough to be said that the insurer is required (by case-law) to prove the allegation of wilful misconduct when he wishes to defend himself against the contention of the assured that the loss caused by barratry.

Peril of the sea

The rule 'he who alleges must prove' also applies to the possible defence of wilful misconduct that the underwriter may use to strike the contention of the assured that the loss proximately caused by a peril of the sea.

ff. Exclusion clause

The insurer bears the onus of proof where the cover is subject to specific exclusions. In case of a reverse burden clause[357], the insurer is required to present an arguable case for the operation of an exclusion and satisfaction of the casual connection required by the policy between the exclusion and the loss.

'It is axiomatic in insurance law, that, as it is always for an insurer to prove an exception, so it is for him to prove the breach of a condition which would relieve him from liability in respect of a particular loss'[358].

c. Which is the required standard of proof?

aa. Higher standard in unexplainable losses

If the insurer wishes to prove that the presumption of loss caused by a peril of the sea (in unexplainable losses) is wrong in a particular case, he has to try harder to persuade the court that something else happened and, therefore, he is not liable to pay the claim of the assured.

The required standard of proof for the insurer is higher than the normal in civil cases (balance of probabilities). It is much more difficult to prove that a presumption is false than to prove that a contention of the plaintiff is false. It follows that the higher standard of proof still operates within the civil case (we do not deal with criminal allegation) and stands somewhere between 'balance of probabilities' and 'beyond reasonable doubt'. I think that it tends to be closer to the 'beyond reasonable doubt' rule, because such presumption needs very strong evidence to be struck down.

---

357 Bennett, p.110.

358 Bond Air Services Ltd v Hill (1955)2 Q.B. 417 at 427 per Goddard L.C.J.

bb. Higher standard in wilful misconduct (fraud)

In Hellas[359], article 388 of the Penal Code makes fraud in relation to insurance a crime. In Britain[360] if the insurer alleges that the assured is a criminal, he must prove it. The question now is: which is the required standard of proof? Unfortunately, there is no absolute legal answer to this question. I would briefly say that the admissibility of a criminal charge in a civil action purports to protect the interests of the individual (here, the underwriter) who alleges it against the other litigant (here, the plaintiff assured). This means that the plaintiff assured will not be sent to jail, if he loses in the civil action. If a criminal charge is made against the assured before a criminal court, the criminal court is not legally bound[361] by the decision of the civil court. To cut a long story short, I would say that it would not be wrong for someone to argue that the required standard (Keramefs[362] deals with the matter in the contest of the civil action) of proof is higher than in any other civil contention, but lower than in any criminal charge in a penal procedure. The criterion of the seriousness of the allegation would be useful, but it seems to me that it is not accurate enough. Again, I believe that the judge will be ready to accept that the assured did a fraud in a civil case only when he is almost sure that the charge is based on truth. I conclude that the higher standard of proof in wilful misconduct also (like in unexplainable losses) tends to be even closer to 'beyond reasonable doubt'.

cc. The balance of probabilities in all other cases

It is suffice to say that in all other defences that the underwriter makes, the 'balance of probabilities' rule apply like in all civil actions[363].

D. The Barratry Problem

There is a strong debate in marine insurance law on the issue whether the assured must prove that barratry occurred without his consent or not. If the insurer is supposed to prove that the assured consented to barratry, this amounts to a criminal charge, namely fraud of the assured on the marine insurance policy. Therefore, the standard of proof is higher than in any other civil case. In 1994[364]

---

[359] Kontaxi, Hellenic Penal Code (in Greek), p.267.

[360] Martin, p.197. Williams, pp.6-45 and in particular pp. 11-14.

[361] Of course, it is taken into consideration. This is the case, at least, under the Hellenic Code of Penal Procedure, Harris (in p.171) deals with this legal issue in the context of the European Convention on Human Rights, article 6 (the right to a fair trial) article 62 (Karras, p.56).

[362] P.108.

[363] Hodges, (in p.253) interprets the rule as 'the event is more likely to have occurred than not'. However, (in p.270) Hodges seems to be confused, because she compares the standard of proof in a civil action to the required standard of proof of a criminal charge in a civil action.

[364] Diggens v Sun Alliance & London Insurance P.L.C (unreported), 9 July 1994 (C.A.) in Bennett, p.327, fn 91.

the courts still felt bound to apply the rule first established in Issaias[365]. They no more require 'beyond reasonable doubt', but they seek for 'the high standard of proof associated with fraud'. Even in cases like Martiartu[366] and Michael[367] reference is made to this high standard, although it was said that the assured bears the burden of proving that he did not consent in barratry. I would try not to propose an absolute solution, but to identify the legal problem and to make clear that a closer examination of it would lead to absolute conclusions. If we accept that the assured bears the onus of proof (without his consent barratry), the usual standard of proof is required: balance of probabilities. If we conclude that the insurer bears the burden of proof (fraud: barratry with consent of the assured) the high standard of proof is then expected. Let us think of a simple case: Assured (A) claims on barratry. Insurer's (I) defence is based on fraud. Firstly, 'A' must prove barratry. Of course, he will try to convince the court that this happened without his consent. If he fails to convince the court that he did consent, then he will fail. Secondly, 'I' must definitely prove fraud. It is out of the question that he will also try to convince the court for the truth of his allegation. He will do his best. Thirdly, in both cases the standard of proof depends on the rules relating to a civil action or a criminal allegation in a civil action. Fourthly, the burden of proof lies with the assured, because of the wording of clause 6.2.5. of the Institute Time Clauses Hulls: barratry is covered *provided....not resulted from want of due diligence by the assured owners, managers*. It is not said 'unless it is proven that barratry resulted from want of due diligence...'. If the wording was as such, it would have been for the insurer to bear the burden of proving fraud of the assured. Therefore, 'A' must prove barratry under the required condition that barratry did not result from his want of due diligence. 'Resulted' seems to be wider than 'proximately caused' and reminds us the wording of section 55(2)a of the Marine Insurance Act 1906 'attributable to' which is also interpreted to be wider to include 'proximate' and 'remote' cause. Hodges[368] makes similar comments on this issue. Finally, if 'A' does not prove that he did not consent, he will fail. If 'A' brings enough evidence that he did not consent, he will discharge the burden of proof. Then, 'I' shall prove that 'A' did consent, still bound by the higher standard of proof.

---

365 Elfie A. Issaias v Marine Insurance Co. (1923) 15 Ll.L.Rep.186.

366 Compania Naviera Martiartu v Royal Exchange Assurance Corp. (The Amus) (1924) 19 Ll.L.Rep.95.

367 Pierman Shipping Co. S.A. v Chester (1979) 1 Lloyd's Rep.55.

368 Pp. 310-311.

E. Other legal aspects

a. How (evidence)?

Evidence tends to prove the existence or non existence of some fact. It may consist of testimony, stories of the crew or master, documentary evidence, real evidence[369]. Direct evidence is not always possible to be adduced, especially of deliberate sinking and complicity. Bennett[370] refers to Issaias, Martiartu, Anghelatos and Ikarian Reefer Cases[371]. This is why circumstantial[372] evidence is admissible in a marine insurance case. Although oral evidence cannot be given to contradict written documents, if there are allegations of fraud, the parole evidence rule is overridden. The aim of this is for the court to best pursue the truth.

b. Joint assured - alternative claims

In almost all the text we discussed the legal issues of burden and standard of proof assuming that there are one plaintiff assured, one defendant insurer, one claim. However, it is possible that owners and mortgagees are insured under the same policy. In Samuel v Dumas[373] it was ruled that the wilful misconduct of the owner did not prejudice the claim of the mortgagee (not party to the fraud) in respect of their interest[374]. Additionally, in almost all cases both the plaintiff and the defendant make alternative claims and not just one.

c. General Average

Rule E of York-Antwerp Rules 1994 provides that 'the onus of proof is upon the party claiming in general average to show that the loss claimed is properly allowable as general average'[375].

---

369 Martin, p.175. Useful comments on this important legal issue are made by Arnould (in p.1139), Colinvaux (in p.161) Goodacre (in pp.34-36), Hodgesfin (in p.247) and Ivamy (in p.169 and p. 233).

370 P. 221.

371 Elfie a. Issaias v Marine Insurance Co. (1923)15 Ll.L.Rep.186 at 187]; [Compania Naviera Martiartu v Royal Exchange Assurance Corpn. (The Arnus) (1924)19 Ll.L.Rep.95 at 96]; [Anghelaxos v Northern Assurance Co. Ltd. (The Olympia) (1924)19 Ll.L.Rep.255 at 257-258]; [Justice Compania Naviera S.A. v Prudential Assurance Co. Ltd. (The Ikavian Reefer) (1995) 1 Lloyd's Rep.455 at 484.

372 Circumstances are best described in Lemos v British & Foreign Marine Insurance Co.Ltd.(1931)39 Ll.L.Rep.275. Bennett (in pp.222-223) offers a long list of it.

373 P. Samuel & Co.Ltd. v Dumas (1924) A.C. 431; (1924) All ER 66; 40 TLR 375; 93 L.J. K.B. 415; 130 L.T. 771; 16 Asp. M.L.C. 305; 29 Com. Cas 239; 18 Ll.Lrep.211.

374 O'May, (in p.114) points out that the interest of the owner and the mortgagee were separately insured, albeit under the same policy.

375 O'May, (in p.364) refers also to 'The Seapool' case (1934) P.53 at 61.

d. Arbitration

Firstly, it must be said that before going to court both parties may choose to refer the dispute to arbitration. A special clause (arbitration clause)[376] may be present in most marine insurance contracts. In such case, it is true that the procedure is more flexible and quicker. In general, however, the rules regarding the burden and standard of proof shall apply. Secondly, the applicant for a stay must adduce evidence that he is ready and willing to refer the dispute to arbitration, but having done so the onus will shift to the plaintiff in the action to show reason why it should not been referred[377].

e. In practice

English judges, with their well trained, patient and gentle touch can be trusted to find out who did it, with quite sufficient certainty by any standard. This does not mean that there is no such thing as a burden of proof[378]. It only becomes crucial, when the judge cannot make up his mind on the evidence, usually because no satisfactory evidence can be found to put before him. That, however, is a rare occasion[379]. On the other hand, the practical importance of the rules regarding onus of proof cannot be underestimated: both the insurer and the assured will be best prepared to prove their case according to the rules regulating burden of proof. Therefore, clarity of these rules is necessary to be established by English courts. Fresh evidence[380] (in the form of diaries of the managing director) was admitted in Ladd v Marshall[381] by the Court of Appeal and approved by the House of Lords in Skone v Skone[382].

Conclusion of Part III

Burden and standard of proof in marine insurance litigation is regulated in a way that both the plaintiff assured and the defendant insurer are equally dealt by law. First, the plaintiff must prove his case. Secondly, the defendant must prove his defence. When he makes a criminal charge (wilful misconduct-Fraud of the assured) the standard of proof is higher than the balance of probabilities which is the standard of proof in any civil action. Clarity of rules in relevance to the criminal matter into a civil litigation is necessary for legal and practical reasons.

---

376 Colinvaux, p.164.

377 Colinvaux, (in p.164) refers to 'Piercy v Young (1879) 14 Ch. D. 200, 209, Hadson v Railway Passengers' Assurance (1882) 9 Q.B.D. 188, 190, Vamelrey v Simpson (1896) 1 Ch. 166 and Skinner v Uzielli (1908)24 T.L.R. 266-267. Clarke, (in p.200) refers to other aspects of arbitration in insurance cases.

378 Colinvaux, p.90.

379 Colinvaux, (in p.90) titles it 'burden of proof: reality of concept'.

380 O'May (in p.112) refers to circumstantial evidence and fresh evidence as the central issues of the hearing in Ladd. Marshall.

381 (1954) 1 W.L.R. 1489 at p.1491.

382 (1971) 1. W.L.R. 812.

It seems to me that the higher standard of proof regarding the defence of wilful misconduct tends to be closer to the rule 'beyond reasonable doubt'. It is said that the heavier the allegation is, the higher the standard goes. In my opinion, the rule is that the higher standard of proof is always higher (and closer to beyond reasonable doubt) in any criminal charge that the insurer makes in order to avoid paying the claim. Of course, evidence and experience shall guide the judges to decide for the assured or the underwriter in each different case. The general rules of burden and standard of proof are not, therefore, regarded as of minor importance.

CONCLUSION

It is not an easy thing to compare United Kingdom law with any other European continental law because common law in United Kingdom is different from civil law in the European continent. In marine insurance law, the Hellenic and the English provisions relating to collision liability insured and abandonment are much different.

First of all, there is a completely different approach of the legal issues arising from collision liability and abandonment. The English legal authors spend pages and pages to explain legal problems that the Hellenic legal authors do not touch. The Hellenic authors stick to legal details which are not commented in the United Kingdom law.

Second, the English courts rarely seem to rule differently over the same legal aspects. For example, we saw such dispute in the legal matter whether the abandoned subject – matter insured becomes *res nullius* if the underwriter does not accept to take over the interest of the assured in whatever may remain of the subject – matter insured. On the contrary, the Hellenic courts often express different views on the same legal issues. Especially in marine insurance, the judgments of the courts are often critiqued by the authors who pursue to produce a secondary source of law. This is why disputes are many and a part of almost every legal aspect. It is, indeed, a rare case that in some issues all the authors and courts agree.

Third, the theoretical approach of marine insurance law in collision liability and abandonment is not sufficient. This is because practice is very important and sometimes, very different from the legal theory. For example, notice of abandonment may be given orally in theory, but in practice this rarely happens. This is why we presented a written sample of notice of abandonment.

Finally, after the closer observation of the difficulties arisen in abandonment under both the Hellenic and the United Kingdom law, we proposed a revision of the current law hoping that it contributes to clarification of the issues in legal theory and in the practice of marine insurance.

BIBLIOGRAPHY (Parts I & II)

[Collision liability, abandonment]

A. United Kingdom

1. Arnould's *Law of Marine Insurance and Average*, Sir Mustill M.J. and Gilman J.C.B., Volume 1, Sixteenth Edition, London, 1981.
2. Balkin R. P., *The establishment and work of the IMO Legal Committee,* Rhodes Academy of Oceans Law and Policy, Promoting the rule of law in the world's oceans, Course Materials, Sixth Session, 9 July to 27 July 2001, Volume 1, Weeks 1 and 2, Thursday, July 12, pp 291-307, Rhodes, Greece, 2001.
3. Beale HG, Bishop WD, Furmstone MP, *Contract, Cases and Materials*, Third Edition, Butterworths, London, Dublin, Edinburgh, 1995.
4. Bennett H., *The Law of Marine Insurance*, Clarendon Press, Oxford, 1996.
5. Birds J., *Modern Insurance Law*, Fourth Edition, Sweet & Maxwell, London, 1997.
6. Brown R.H., *Marine Insurance Vol.1-Principles & Basic Practice*, Fifth Edition, Witherby & Co.Ltd., London, 1986.
7. Carver's *Carriage By Sea*, Colinvaux R., Thirteenth Edition, Steven & Sons London, 1982.
8. Colinvaux R., *The Law of Insurance,* Fifth Edition, Sweet & Maxwell, London, 1984.
9. Cushman J. H., *Collisions in the Black Sea, 2 Soviet warships reportedly nudge US Navy vessels,* The New York Times, p. 1, April 3, 1988, Materials in Rhodes Academy of Oceans Law and Policy, Promoting the rule of law in the world's oceans, Course Materials, Sixth Session, 9 July to 27 July 2001, Volume 2, Week 3, Rhodes, Greece, 2001.
10. Goodacre K., *Marine Insurance Claims*, Witherby & Co. Ltd., London, 1981.
11. Grime P.P., *Shipping Law*, Sweet & Maxwell, London, 1978.
12. Hill C., *Maritime Law, Fourth Edition*, Lloyd's of London Press Ltd, London, New York, Hamburg, Hong Kong, 1995.
13. Hodges S., *Law of Marine Insurance*, Cavendish Publishing Limited, London, 1996.
14. Ivamy E.R.H., *Marine Insurance,* Fourth Edition, Butterworths Insurance Library, Butterworths, London, 1985.
15. Martin E.A., *A Dictionary of Law,* Fourth Edition, Oxford University Press, Oxford, New York, 1997.
16. McKendrik E., *Contract Law,* Third edition, MacMillan Press Ltd, Houndmills, Basingstoke, Hampshire and London, 1997.
17. O' May D., *Marine Insurance, Law and Policy*, Sweet and Maxwell, London, 1993.

18. Oral N., *Oil and water: Caspian oil and transportation challenges facing the Turkish straits,* Rhodes Academy of Oceans Law and Policy, Promoting the rule of law in the world's oceans, Course Materials, Sixth Session, 9 July to 27 July 2001, Volume 2, Week 3, Thursday, July 26, pp 1-19, Rhodes, Greece, 2001.
19. Scmitthoff C.M., *Schmitthoff's Export Trade, The law and practice of international trade*, Steven & Sons, London, 1990.
20. Soons A. H. A., *The effects of a rising sea level on maritime limits and boundaries,* Netherlands International Law Review (1990), pp. 207-232.
21. Thomas R.D., *The Modern Law of Marine Insurance*, LLP, London, New York, Hong-Kong, 1996.
22. Wight R., *Lecture* 5 /3 /99, School of Law, University of Essex, 1999.
23. Wilson J., *Carriage of Goods by Sea*, Second Edition, Financial Time Management, Pitman Publishing, London, 1993.

B. Hellenic

1. Achis H.G., *War risk in Marine Insurance*, Athens, 1952.
2. Antapasis A. M., *Code of Private Maritime Law,* Second Edition, Ant. N. Sakkoulas Publications, Athens, Komotini, 1991.
3. Argyriadis A.A., *Elements of Insurance Law*, Fourth Edition, Sakkoulas Publications, Thessaloniki, 1986.
4. Athens News Agency, *Collision between two ferry boats,* Metrorama, p. 7, Athens, 6 February, 2004.
5. Athens News Agency, *Nine seamen were saved after abandonment of a ship,* Metrorama, p. 3, Athens, 21 April, 2001.
6. Balis G., *General Principles (of Civil Law)*, Eighth Edition, Athens, 1961.
7. Doukas S.I., *The Private Insurance*, Second Edition, Athens, 1988.
8. Hatzinikolaou – Agelidou R., *Liability insurance and especially the compulsory liability insurance in motor vehicle accidents*, Ant. N. Sakkoulas Publications, Athens, Komotini, 1998.
9. Kalantzis A.K., *The law of private insurance*, Nomiki Bibliothiki, Athens, 1988.
10. Karavas V, *Manual of Commercial Law*, Athens, 1962.
11. Kiantos V, *Marine Insurance of Cargo*, Sakkoulas Publications, Thessaloniki, 1982.
12. Kiantos D.V, *Insurance Law*, Sixth Edition, Sakkoulas Publications, Thessaloniki, 1998.
13. Kiantou-Pampouki A., *Maritime Law*, Third Edition, Ant. N. Sakkoulas Publications, Athens, Thessaloniki, 1993.
14. Kritikou A.G., *Indemnity in Car Accidents*, Athens, 1987.
15. Papamichalopoulos N., *Carriage of goods by sea*, Athens, 1956.

16.Papapolitis N.I., *Insurance of the Liability of the Shipowner*, Athens, 1957.
17.Rokas I.K., *Private Insurance*, Sixth Edition, Ant. N. Sakkoulas Publications, Athens, 1998.
18.Rokas K., *Lessons of Commercial Law*, Second Volume, Athens, 1972.
19.Sarlis P., *The institution of abandonment in the Code of Private Maritime Law (KINΔ)*, EEΔ 157, 1963.
20.Skantzakis A.P., *Insurance Lessons*, Athens, 1970.
21.Skouloudis Z., *Law of Private Insurance*, Second Edition, P. Sakkoulas Brothers Publications, Santaroza 1d, Athens, 1995.
22.Spiliopoulos K., *Elements of Maritime Law (University Lectures)*, Athens, 1967.
23.Stamelos C., *English Legal Terminology*, Nomiki Bibliothiki, Athens, 2006.
24.TO BHMA (To Vima, The Step), *The cruise "was wrecked" in the English Channel*, p. A8 (International News), 25th of August 1999.

BIBLIOGRAPHY (Part III)

[Burden of Proof]

A. United Kingdom

1. Arnould's *Law of Marine Insurance and Average*, Sir Mustill M.J. and Gilman J.C.B., Volume 1, Sixteenth Edition, London, 1981.
2. Beale HG, Bishop WD, Furmstone MP, *Contract, Cases and Materials*, Third Edition, Butterworths, London, Dublin, Edinburgh, 1995.
3. Bennett H., *The Law of Marine Insurance,* Clarendon Press, Oxford, 1996.
4. Birds J., *Modern Insurance Law*, Fourth Edition, Sweet and Maxwell, London, 1997.
5. Botes J. H., *From good faith to utmost good faith in Marine Insurance,* Peter Lang GmbH, Frankfurt am Main, Berlin, Bern, Bruxelles, New York, Oxford, Wien, 2006.
6. Brown R. H., *Marine Insurance Vol.1-Principles & Basic Practice*, Fifth Edition, Witherby & Co.Ltd., London, 1986.
7. Bugg S.G.,Simon H., *Fachwörterbuch, Kompakt, Recht, Englisch, Englisch-Deutsch, Deutsch-Englisch,* Alpmann Schmidt, Münster, Langenscheidt, Berlin, München, Wien, Zürich, New York, 2006.
8. Carver's *Carriage By Sea*, Colinvaux R., Thirteenth Edition, Steven & Sons London, 1982.
9. Clarke M., *Policies and Perceptions of Insurance, An Introduction to Insurance Law*, Clarendon Press, Oxford, 1997.
10. Classen C.D., *Europa-Recht, Verträge zur Gründung der Europäischen Gemeinscahften, Vertrag über die Europäische Union, Charta der Gründrechte der Europäischen Union, Rechtsstellung des Unionsbürgers,*

Verfahrensordnungen,Satzung des Europarates, Menschenrechtskonvention, Europa-wahl Gesetz, Europaabgeordneten Gesetz, 21. Neubearbeitete Auflage, Beck, Deutscher Taschenbuch Verlag GmbH, München, 2006.
11.CNN, *US Navy Submarine collides with Japanese Fishing Vessel; 10 still missing,* Breaking News, www.cnn.com, February 9, 2001.
12.Colinvaux R., *The Law of Insurance*, Fifth Edition, Sweet and Maxwell, London, 1984.
13.Foster N. G., *Blackstone's EC Legislation,* Ninth Edition, Blackstone Press Limited, London, 1998-9.
14.Goodacre K., *Marine Insurance Claims*, Witherby & Co. Ltd., London, 1981.
15.Harris DJ, O' Boyle M, Warbrick C, *Law of the European Convention on Human Rights*, Butterworths, London, Dublin, Edinburgh, 1995.
16.Hodges S., *Law of Marine Insurance*, Cavendish Publishing Limited, London, 1996.
17.Ivamy E.R.H., *Marine Insurance*, Fourth Edition, Butterworths Insurance Library, Butterworths, London, 1985.
18.Köhler H., *Bürgerliches Gesetzbuch,* 58. Überarbeitete Auflage, Beck, Deutscher Taschenbuch Verlag GmbH, München, 2006.
19.Leg N., *Proof of wilful casting away, The Ikarian Reefer*, LMCLQ (1989), pp. 305-308.
20.Martin E.A., *A Dictionary of Law*, Fourth Edition, Oxford University Press, Oxford, New York, 1997
21.McKendrik E., *Contract Law,* Third edition, MacMillan Press Ltd, Houndmills, Basingstoke, Hampshire and London, 1997.
22.Medicus D., *Bürgerliches Recht,* 20. Neubearbeitete Auflage, Carl Heymanns Verlag, Köln, Berlin, München, 2004.
23.Muchlinski P.T., *The Captain Panagos D.P.*, LMCLQ (1989), pp.25-27.
24.O' May D., *Marine Insurance, Law and Policy*, Sweet and Maxwell, London, 1993.
25.Palandt O., *Bürgerliches Gesetzbuch,* Beck' sche Kurz Kommentare, Band 7, 66. Auflage, Verlag C. H. Beck, München, 2007.
26.Satzger H., *Internationales und Europäisches Strafrecht,* Nomos Verlagsgesellschaft, Baden Baden, 2005.
27.Scmitthoff C.M., *Schmitthoff's Export Trade, The law and practice of international trade*, Steven & Sons, London, 1990.
28.Thomas R.D., *The Modern Law of Marine Insurance*, LLP, London, New York, Hong-Kong, 1996.
29.Tröndle H., Fischer T., *Strafgesetzbuch und Nebengesetze,* Beck' sche Kurz Kommentare, Band 10, 54. Auflage, Verlag C. H. Beck, München, 2007.

30. Weigend T., *Strafgesetzbuch, Mit Einführungsgesetz, Völkerstrafgesetzbuch, Wirtschaftsstrafgesetz, Betäubungsmittelgesetz, Versammlungsgesetz,* 42. Auflage, Beck, Deutscher Taschenbuch Verlag GmbH, München, 2006.
31. Williams K.S., *Textbook of Criminology*, Third Edition, Blackstone Press Limited, London, 1997.

B. Hellenic

1. Achis H.G., *War risk in Marine Insurance*, Athens, 1952.
2. Androulakis N.K., *Fundamental principles of the penal procedure*, Second Edition, 1994.
3. Dagtoglou P.D., *Civil Rights, A'*, Ant. N. Sakkoulas Publications, Athens, Athens-Komotini, 1991.
4. Karras A., *Penal Procedural Law*, Ant. N. Sakkoulas Publications, Athens, Athens-Komotini, 1994.
5. Keramefs K.D., *Civil Procedural Law*, Second Edition, Ant. N. Sakkoulas Publications, Athens, Thessaloniki, 1986.
6. Kiantos V, *Marine Insurance of Cargo*, Sakkoulas Publication, Thessaloniki, 1982.
7. Kiantou-Pampouki A., *Maritime Law*, Third Edition, Ant. N. Sakkoulas Publications, Athens, Thessaloniki, 1993.
8. Kontaxi A.K., *Penal Code*, P. Sakkoulas, Santa Rosa 1d-Athens, 1995.
9. Papapolitis N.I., *Insurance of the Shipowner*, Athens, 1957, Athens, Komotini, 1985.
10. Rokas 1.K., *Private Insurance*, Sixth Edition, Ant. N. Sakkoulas Publications, Athens, 1998.
11. Scandamis N., *European Law, Texts, I. Treaties – Unified,* Ant. N. Sakkoulas Publications, Athens, Komotini, 2003.
12. Spyridakis I. S., *General Principles (of Civil Law),* Ant. N. Sakkoulas Publication, Athens, Komotini, 1985.
13. Stamelos C., *English Legal Terminology,* Nomiki Bibliothiki, Athens, 2006.

LIST OF CASES (Parts I & II)

[Collision liability, abandonment]

A. United Kingdom

Aldridge v Bell (1816) 1 Stark 498

Allgemeine Versicherungs – Gesellschaft Helvetia v Administrator of German Property (1931) 1 KB 672, CA

AG v Glen Line Ltd and the Liverpool and London War Risks Insurance Association Ltd (1930) 37 Ll L Rep 55, HL

Arrow Shipping Co Ltd v Tyne Improvement Commissioners (*The Crystal*) (1894) AC 508, HL

Becker, Gray v London Assurance (1918) AC 101

Bennett Steamship Co v Hull Mutual Steamship Protecting Society (1914) 3 KB 57

Bradley v H Newson, Sons & Co (1919) AC 16

Chandler v Blogg (1898) 1 QB 32

Costain – Blankevoort (UK) Dredging Co Ltd v Davenport (The Nassau Bay) (1979) 1 Lloyd's Rep 395

Curie & Co v Bombay Native Insurance Co (1869) LR 3 PC 72

Firma C – Trade SA v Newcastle Protection & Indemnity Association (*The Fanti*) (1989) 1 Lloyd's Rep 239

Forest Land, Timber & Railways Co Ltd v Rickards and other Test Cases (1941) 70 Ll L Rep 173

Furness Withy & Co Ltd v Duder (1936) 55 Ll L Rep 52; 2 All ER 119, KBD; 2 KB 461

Gas Float Whitton No.2 (1897) AC 337

George Cohen, Sons & Co v Standard Marine Insurance Co (1925) 30 Com Cas 139, KBD

Gernon v Royal Exchange Assurance (1815) 6 Taunt 383

Hall Brothers Steamship Co v Young (The Trident) (1939) 1 KB 748; 1 All ER 809, CA

Hough v Head (1885) 52 LT 861

Hunt v Royal Exchange Assurance (1816) 5 M & S 47

Irving v Manning (1847) 1 HL Cas 287

Jardine v Leathley (1863) 32 LJQB 132

Kaltenbach v Mackenzie (1878) 3 CPD 467

Mancomunidad del Vapor Frumiz v Royal Exchange Assurance (1927) 1 KB 567

Marstrand Fishing Co Ltd v Beer (The Girl Pat) (1936) 56 Ll L Rep 163; (1937) 1 All ER 158

Mayor & Corp of Boston v France, Fenwick & Co Ltd (1923) 15 Ll L Rep 85; 28 Com Cas 367

McCowan v Baine & Johnston (*The Niobe*) (1891) AC 401

Merchants Marine Insurance Co v North of England P & I Association (1926) 32 Com Cas 165; 26 Ll L Rep 201

Norwich Union Fire Insurance Society Ltd v William H Price Ltd (1934) AC 455

Oceanic Steam Navigation Co v Evans (1934) 50 Ll L Rep 1, CA; 40 Com Cas 108, CA

Owners of Cargo ex Greystoke Castle v Owners of Cheldale (Morrison Steamship Co Ltd) (1947) AC 265; 80 Ll L Rep 55 HL (affirming The Cheldale (1945) P 10; 78 Ll L Rep 129)

Parmeter v Todhunter (1808) 1 Camp 541

Pelton Steamship Co Ltd v (The Zelo) (1925) 22 Ll L Rep 510, KBD

Pesquerias y Secaderos de Bacalao de Espana SA v Beer (1946) 79 Ll L Rep 417, KBD

Polurrian Steamship Co v Young (1915) 1 KB 1922; All ER 116; 20 Com Cas 152

Polpen Shipping Co Ltd v Commercial Union Assurance Co Ltd (1943) 1 All ER 162

Rankin v Potter (1873) LR 6, HL

Re Margetts and Ocean Accident and Guarantee Corp (1901) 2 KB 792

Re Nautilus Steam Shipping Co Ltd (1935) 52 Ll L Rep 183

Reischer v Borwick (1894) 2 QB 548

Rickards v Forestal Land, Timber & Railways Co (The Minden) (1942) AC 50

Rotch v Edie (1795) 6 TR 413

Roux v Salvador (1836) 3 Bing (NC) 266

Russian Bank for Foreign Trade v Excess Insurance Co Ltd (1918) 2 KB 123; (1919) 1 KB 39, CA; 24 Com Cas 55; 35 TLR 42

Ruys v Royal Exchange Assurance Co (1897) 2 QB 135

Sea Insurance Co v Hadden (1884) 13 QBD 706

Simpson & Co v Thompson (1877) 3 App Cas 279

Socony Mobil Oil Co Inc v West of England Ship Owners Mutual Insurance Association (London) Ltd (*The Padre Island*) (1984) 1 Lloyd's Rep 408

Socony Mobil Oil Co Inc v West of England Ship Owners Mutual Insurance Association (London) Ltd (*The Padre Island*) (No 2) (1990) 2 Lloyd's Rep 191, HL

Stewart v Greenock Marine Insurance Co (1848) 2 HL Cas 159

Stoomvart Maatschappij Nederland v P & O Steam Navigation Co (*The Khedive*) (1882) 7 App Cas 795

The Bamburi (1982) 1 Lloyd's Rep 312

The Bramley Moore (1963) 2 Lloyd's Rep 429

The London Steamship Owners' Mutual Insurance Association v The Grampian Steamship Co (*The Balnacraig*) (1889) 24 QBD 663
The Robertson (1939) AC 371, HL
The Sanday Case (1916) 1 AC 650, HL
The Vandyck (1887) 7 PD 42
Thomas Wilson, Sons & Co v Owners of the Cargo per the Xantho (*The Xantho*) (1887) 12 App Cas 503.
Thompson v Reynolds (1857) 26 LJQB 93
Union Marine Insurance Co v Borwick (1898) 2 QB 279
Uzielli v Boston Marine Insurance Co (1884) 15 QBD 11, CA.
Vacuum Oil Co v Union Insurance Society of Canton (1926) 25 Ll L Rep 546, CA
William France Fenwick & Co Ltd v Merchants Marine Insurance Co Ltd (1915) 3 KB 290, CA
Woodley & Co v Mitchell & Co (1883) 11 QBD 47
Xenos v Fox (1868) LR 3; CP 630; 17 WR 893

B. United States

The North Star (1882) 106 US 17
The Virginia Dollar (1925) 149 US 39

C. Hellenic

Supreme Courts

Areios Pagos[*] (ΑΠ) 347 / 1938, 50 (Ν΄) Θ 161
Council of State[**] (ΣτΕ) 63 / 1953, 4 (Δ΄) ΕΕΔ 65
Areios Pagos (ΑΠ) 146 / 1973, 21 NoB 899
Areios Pagos (ΑΠ) 213 / 1982, 30 NoB 1266
Areios Pagos (ΑΠ) 1246 / 2003, Review of Maritime Law (ΕΝΔ) 32 (2004) 1
Areios Pagos (ΑΠ) 1651 / 2005, Review of Maritime Law (ΕΝΔ) 33 (2005) 241

Courts of Appeal

Athens Court of Appeal (ΕφΑθ) 1444 / 1954, 65 (ΞΕ΄) Θ 1026
Athens Court of Appeal (ΕφΑθ) 1011 / 1968, 19 (ΙΘ΄) ΕΕΔ 403
Athens Court of Appeal (ΕφΑθ) 2234 / 1974, 2 (Β΄) (1974) ΕπΣυγκΔ 254
Thessaloniki Court of Appeal (ΕφΘεσ) 156 / 1979, (1980) Αρμ (Armenopoulos, Periodical) 565
Athens Court of Appeal (ΕφΑθ) 1760 / 1981, 22 ΕλλΔικ 637

* Supreme Court for Civil and Penal Cases.
** Supreme Court for Administrative Cases.

Athens Court of Appeal (ΕφΑθ) 6191 / 1981, 33 (ΛΓ΄) ΕΕΔ 263
Athens Court of Appeal (ΕφΑθ) 3245 / 1985, 13 (ΙΓ΄) (1985) ΕπΣυγκΔ 400
Athens Court of Appeal (ΕφΑθ) 4326 / 1985, 37 ΕΕΔ 113
Athens Court of Appeal (ΕφΑθ) 4936 / 1985, 26 ΕλλΔικ 958
Piraeus Court of Appeal 682 / 2004, Review of Maritime Law (ΕΝΔ) 32 (2004) 434
Piraeus Court of Appeal (ΕφΠειρ) 1141 / 2004, Review of Maritime Law (ΕΝΔ) 32 (2004) 440
Piraeus Court of Appeal (ΕφΠειρ) 62 / 2005, Review of Maritime Law (ΕΝΔ) 33 (2005) 256
Piraeus Court of Appeal (ΕφΠειρ) 289 / 2005, Review of Maritime Law (ΕΝΔ) 33 (2005) 196
Piraeus Court of Appeal (ΕφΠειρ) 704 / 2005, Review of Maritime Law (ΕΝΔ) 33 (2005) 247
Piraeus Court of Appeal (ΕφΠειρ) 773 / 2005, Review of Maritime Law (ΕΝΔ) 34 (2006) 20

Courts of First Instance

Piraeus Court of First Instance (ΠΠΠειρ) 201 / 1921, 22 (ΛΒ΄) Θ 137
Piraeus Court of First Instance (ΠΠΠειρ) 774 / 1928, 6 (ΣΤ΄) Δικ 126
Athens Court of First Instance (ΠΠΑθ) 9425 / 1966, 17 (ΙΖ΄) ΕΕΔ 414
Corinth Court of First Instance (ΠΠΚορ) 306 / 1969, (1969) Αρμ (Armenopoulos, Periodical) 778
Athens Court of First Instance (ΠΠΑθ) 6988 / 1971, 39 (1972) Paper of Hellenes Lawyers (EEN, Efimeris Ellinon Nomikon) 87
Thessaloniki Court of First Instance (ΠΠΘεσ) 2177 / 1978, 8 (Η΄) (1980) ΕπΣυγκΔ 342
Athens Court of First Instance (ΠΠΑθ) 3831 / 1979, 10 ΕΝΔ 30
Piraeus Court of First Instance (ΠΠΠειρ) 4883 / 2004, Review of Maritime Law (ΕΝΔ) 32 (2004) 438
Piraeus Court of First Instance (ΜΠΠειρ) 5794 / 2005, Review of Maritime Law (ΕΝΔ) 34 (2006), 30

List Of Cases (Part III)

[Burden of Proof]

A. United Kingdom

Banco de Barcelona and Others v Union Marine Insurance Co Ltd (1925) 30 Com Cas 316
Bater v Bater [1951] P. 35

Bond Air Services Ltd v Hill (1955) 2 QB 417
Boston Fruit 6 v British and Foreign Mar. Ins. 6. [1905] 1 KB 637
Compania Maritima of Barcelona v Wishart (1918) 23 Com Cas 264
Compania Naviera *Martiartu* v Royal Exchange Assurance Corp. (The Arnus), (1923) K.B. 650; (1924) 19 Ll L Rep 95
Compania Naviera Santi SA v Indemnity Marine Insurance co Ltd (*Tropaio-foros*) (1960) 2 Lloyd's Rep 469
Continental Illinois National Bank and Trust Co. of Chicago v Alliance Assurance Co. Ltd (1986) 2 Lloyd's Rep 470
De Marco and Gazan v Scottish Metropolitan Assurance Co (1923) 14 Ll L Rep 173
Diggens v Sun Alliance & London Insurance p.I.c (unreported), 9 July 1994 CA
Elfie A. *Issaias* v Marine Insurance Co. Ltd. (1923) 15 Ll L Rep 186
Empire SS Co Ins. v Co (1925) 22 Ll L Rep 437
Euterpe SS Co Ltd v North of England Protecting and Indemnity Association Ltd (1917) 33 TLR 540, KBD
General Steam Navigation Co Ltd. v Janson *(1915)* 31 TLR 630, KBD
General Steam Navigation Co v R *(1927)* 27 Ll L Rep 366, KBD
Gibson v Small (1853) 4 HL Cas 353
Golodetz and Co. Inc. v Gzarnikow - Rionda Co.Inc. (1980) 1 WLR 495
Graham Joint Stock Shipping Co. V Merchants' Mar. Ins. Co. [1923] 1 KB 592
Green v Brown (1744) 2 Str. 1 199
Hoffmann & Co v British General Insurance Co. (1922) 10 Ll L Rep 434
Ladd v Marshall (1954) 1 WLR 1459
Lamb Head Shipping Co Ltd v Jennings (*The Marel*) (1992) 1 Lloyd's Rep 402
Lemos v British &Foreign Marine Insurance Co. Ltd (1931) 39 Ll L Rep 275
Macbeth & Co. v King (1916) 86 LJKB 1004, KBD
Magnus v Buttemer (1924) AC 431
Michelos & Sons Maritime SA v Prudential Assurance Co. Ltd. (*The Zinovia*) (1984) 2 Lloyd's Rep 264
Miceli v Union Marine & General Insurance Co Ltd (1938), Co Ll L Rep 275
Mitrovich Bros. & Co v Merchants Marine Insurance Co. Ltd (1923) 14 Ll L Rep 25
Munro Brice & Co v FW Marten (1920) 2 Ll L Rep 25
National Justice Compania Naviera SA v Prudential Assurance Co Ltd (*The Ikarian Reefer*), (1993) 2 Lloyd's Rep 68; (1995) 1 Lloyd's Rep 455
Parker v Potts (1815) 3 Dow 23
Piermay Shipping Co. SA and Brandt's Ltd v Chester (*The Michael*) (1979) 1 Lloyd's Rep 55; (1979) 2 Lloyd's Rep 1 CA
Regina Fur Co Ltd v Bossay (1958) 2 Lloyd's Rep 425
Rhesa Shipping Co.SA v Edmunds (*The Popi M*) (1985) 2 Lloyd's Rep 1; (1985) 1 WLR 948; (1985) 2 All ER 712
Samuel & Co. Ltd v Dumas (1924) AC 431; (1924) All ER 66; 93 LJKB 415

Skandia Insurance Co. Ltd. v Skoljarev (1979) 26 ALR
Skone v Skone (1971) 1 WLR 812
Slattery v Mance (1962) 1 All ER 525
Stebbing v Liverpool & London & Globe (1917) 2 KB 433
Tempus Shipping Co Ltd v Dreyfus & Co Ltd (1930) 1 KB 699
United Scottish Insurance Co. Ltd v British Fishing Vessel Mutual War Risks Association Ltd: *The Braconbush* (1944) 78 Ll L Rep 70, KBD
Yangtsze Ins. Ass. v Lukmanjee[1918] AC 585 (PC)
Zachariassen v Importers' and Exporters' Marine Insurance Co Ltd (1923) 18 Ll L Rep 98, CA

B. *United States*

Commercial Molasses v New York Tank; Barge Co. (1941) 314 U.S. 104

Legislation

Numbers refer to pages

A. UK

The Carriage of Goods by Sea Act 1971 [36, 92]

The Fatal Accidents Act 1976 [36]

The Road Traffic Act 1988
- Section 143 [36]
- Section 145 [36]
- Section 149 [36]

The Contracts (Applicable Law) Act 1990

B. Hellenic

Code of Private Maritime Law (KINΔ)
- Article 1 [24, 25, 112, 115]
- Articles 84-106 [37]
- Article 84 [40]
- Articles 235-245 [25]
- Article 235 [23, 39, 112, 115]
- Article 236 [112, 115]
- Article 245 [112, 115]
- Articles 257-288 [25]
- Article 269 [11, 22, 23, 25, 37-41, 112, 115]
- Article 272 [22, 25, 113, 115]
- Article 274 [23, 113, 116]
- Article 276 [113, 116]
- Articles 278-279 [37]
- Article 280 [47, 113, 116]
- Articles 281-288 [47]
- Article 281 [47-51, 62, 63, 113, 116]
- Article 282 [49, 62, 113, 116]
- Article 283 [49, 62, 64, 66, 114, 116]
- Article 284 [60-62, 64, 65, 114, 116]
- Article 285 [63-67, 114, 117]
- Article 287 [63, 64, 67, 114, 117]
- Article 288 [49, 62, 66, 114, 117]

Civil Code
- Article 173 [39, 126]
- Article 200 [39, 126]
- Article 281 [25, 39, 126]
- Article 288 [39]

Penal Code
- Article 388 [85]

Law Decree 551 / 1970 (as amended by the Presidential Decree 118 / 1985)
- Article 1 [23-26]

Law 314 / 1976
- Article 1 [41]

Law 489 / 1976
- Article 6 [40]
- Article 10 [39]

Decree 16560 / 1938
- Article 1 [41]
- Article 9 [41]

C. German

Bürgerliches Gesetzbuch (German Civil Code)
- Artikel 318 [82, 126]

Strafgesetzbuch (German Penal Code)
- Artikel 263 [83, 126]

European Community – European Union Legislation

The 1957 Rome Treaty on European Community [the EC Treaty]
- Article 280 (ex-article 209A) [83]

The 1992 Maastricht Treaty on European Union
- Article Z.77 (amending article 290A of the EC Treaty) [83]

The 1996 Amsterdam Treaty
- Article 2.52 (amending article 290A of the EC Treaty) [83]

Council Directive 73 / 239 / EEC (24.07.1973)

Council Regulation 44 / 2001 (applying in the European Community the Brussels Convention on Jurisdiction and the Enforcement of Judgments in Civil and Commercial Matters 1968)

International Conventions

The Brussels International Collision Convention 1910 [20, 22, 23, 26]
- Article 2 [27, 40]
- Proceedings of Session 18 September to 8 October 1909 [26]

The International Convention on the Inter-governmental Maritime Consultative Organization 1948 [20]

The Rome Convention for the Protection of Human Rights and Fundamental Freedoms 1950 [85, 94]

The Brussels Convention on Jurisdiction and the Enforcement of Judgments in Civil and Commercial Matters 1968

The International Convention on Civil Liability for Oil Pollution Damage 1969 [36]
- Article VII [41]

The International Convention on the Establishment of an International Fund for Compensation for Oil Pollution Damage 1971 [37]

The International Convention on Limitation of Liability in Maritime Claims 1976 [28]

The Rome Convention on the Law Applicable to Contractual Obligations 1980

The International Convention on Salvage 1989 [37]

The York-Antwerp Rules 1994 [87]

Appendix I
The Marine Insurance Act 1906

Section 1
A contract of marine insurance is a contract whereby the insurer undertakes to indemnify the assured in manner and to the extent thereby agreed, against marine losses, that is to say, the losses incident to marine adventure.

Section 39
(1) In a voyage policy there is an implied warranty that at the commencement of the voyage the ship shall be seaworthy for the purpose of the particular adventure insured. [...]
(5) In a time policy there is no implied warranty that the ship shall be seaworthy at any stage of the adventure, but where, with the privity of the assured, the ship is sent to sea in an unseaworthy state, the insurer is not liable for any loss attributable to unseaworthiness.

Section 41
There is an implied warranty that the adventure insured is a lawful one, and that, so far as the assured can control the matter, the adventure shall be carried out in a lawful manner.

Section 55
(1) Subject to the provisions of this Act, and unless the policy otherwise provides, the insurer is liable for any loss proximity caused by a peril insured against, but, subject as aforesaid, he is not liable for any loss which is not proximately caused by a peril insured against.
(2) In particular, (a) the insurer is not liable for any loss attributable to the wilful misconduct of the assured [...]

Section 56
(1) A loss may be either total or partial. Any loss other than a total loss, as hereinafter defined, is a partial loss.
(2) A total loss may be either an actual total loss, or a constructive total loss.
(3) Unless a different intention appears from the terms of the policy, an insurance against total loss includes a constructive, as well as an actual, total loss.
(4) Where the assured brings an action for a total loss and the evidence proves only a partial loss, he may, unless the policy otherwise provides, recover for a partial loss.

Section 57
(1) Where the subject-matter insured is destroyed, or so damaged as to cease to be a thing of the kind insured, or where the assured is irretrievably deprived thereof, there is an actual total loss.
(2) In the case of an actual total loss no notice of abandonment need be given.

Section 58
Where the ship concerned in the adventure is missing, and after the lapse of a reasonable time no news of her has been received, an actual total loss may be presumed.

Section 60
(1) Subject to any express provision in the policy, there is a constructive total loss where the subject-matter insured is reasonably abandoned on account of its actual total loss appearing to be unavoidable or because it could not be preserved from actual total loss without an expenditure which would exceed its value when the expenditure had been incurred.
(2) In particular, there is a constructive total loss (i) Where the assured is deprived of the possession of his ship or goods by a peril insured against, and (a) it is unlikely that he can recover the ship or goods, as the case may be, or (b) the cost of recovering the ship or goods, as the case may be, would exceed their value when recovered; or (ii) In the case of damage to a ship, where she is so damaged by a peril insured against that the cost of repairing the damage would exceed the value of the ship when repaired. In estimating the cost of repairs, no deduction is to be made in respect of general average contributions to those repairs payable by other interests, but account is to be taken of the expense of future salvage operations and of any future general average contributions to which the ship would be liable if repaired; or (iii) In the case of damage to goods, where the cost of repairing the damage and forwarding the goods to their destination would exceed their value on arrival.

Section 61
Where there is a constructive total loss the assured may either treat the loss as a partial loss, or abandon the subject-matter insured to the insurer and treat the loss as if it were an actual total loss.

Section 62
(1) Subject to the provisions of this section, where the assured elects to abandon the subject-matter insured to the insurer, he must give notice of abandonment. If he fails to do so the loss can only be treated as a partial loss.
(2) Notice of abandonment may be given in writing, or by word of mouth, or partly in writing and partly by word of mouth, and may be given in any terms

which indicate the intention of the assured to abandon his insured interest in the subject-matter insured unconditionally to the insurer.
(3) Notice of abandonment must be given with reasonable diligence after the receipt of reliable information of the loss, but where the information is of a doubtful character the assured is entitled to a reasonable time to make inquiry.
(4) Where notice of abandonment is properly given, the rights of the assured are not prejudiced by the fact that the insurer refuses to accept the abandonment.
(5) The acceptance of an abandonment may be either express or implied from the conduct of the insurer. The mere silence of the insurer after notice is not an acceptance.
(6) Where notice of abandonment is accepted the abandonment is irrevocable. The acceptance of the notice conclusively admits liability for the loss and the sufficiency of notice.
(7) Notice of abandonment is unnecessary where, at the time when the assured receives information of the loss, there would be no possibility of benefit to the insurer if notice were given to him.
(8) Notice of abandonment may be waived by the insurer.
(9) Where an insurer has re-insured his risk, no notice of abandonment need be given by him.

Section 63
(1) Where there is a valid abandonment the insurer is entitled to take over the interest of the assured in whatever may remain of the subject-matter insured, and all proprietary rights incidental thereto.
(2) Upon the abandonment of a ship, the insurer thereof is entitled to any freight in course of being earned, and which is earned by her subsequent to the casualty causing the loss, less the expenses of earning it incurred after the casualty; and, where the ship is carrying the owner's goods, the insurer is entitled to a reasonable remuneration for the carriage of them subsequent to the casualty causing the loss.

Section 88
Where by this Act any reference is made to reasonable time, reasonable premium, or reasonable diligence, the question what is reasonable is a question of fact.

Section 93
This Act shall come into operation on the first day of January one thousand nine hundred and seven.

Section 94
This Act may be cited as the Marine Insurance Act, 1906.

APPENDIX II
THE HELLENIC CODE OF PRIVATE MARITIME LAW (KINΔ)

Τίτλος πρώτος
Περί πλοίων και πλοιοκτησίας

Άρθρο 1
Πλοίον, κατά την έννοιαν του παρόντος νόμου, είναι παν σκάφος, χωρητικότητος καθαράς τουλάχιστον δέκα κόρων προωρισμένον όπως κινήται αυτοδυνάμως εν θαλάσση.
Αι διατάξεις του τρίτου, τετάρτου, έκτου, εβδόμου, δωδεκάτου, δεκάτου τρίτου και δεκάτου τετάρτου τίτλων του παρόντος νόμου εφαρμόζονται αναλόγως και επί παντός άλλου πλωτού ναυπηγήματος.

Τίτλος δωδέκατος
Περί συγκρούσεως πλοίων

Άρθρο 235
Επί συγκρούσεως πλοίων, εάν αύτη συνέβη εκ τυχαίου συμβεβηκότος ή ανωτέρας βίας ή εάν υφίσταται αμφιβολία περί των αιτίων της, αι ζημίαι βαρύνουν τους υποστάντας αυτάς.

Άρθρο 236
Εάν η σύγκρουσις συνέβη υπαιτιότητι του ενός των πλοίων αι εντεύθεν ζημίαι βαρύνουν το υπαίτιον πλοίον.
Εν περιπτώσει κοινής υπαιτιότητος έκαστον πλοίον ευθύνεται αναλόγως του βαθμού της βαρυνούσης αυτό υπαιτιότητος.
Εάν δεν δύναται να καθορισθή η αναλογία ή εν ισότητι υπαιτιότητος, η ευθύνη μερίζεται κατ' ίσα μέρη.

Άρθρο 245
Αι διατάξεις του παρόντος τίτλου εφαρμόζονται και επί συγκρούσεως πλοίων καίτοι ηγκυροβολημένων.

Τίτλος δέκατος τέταρτος
Περί θαλασσίας ασφαλίσεως

Άρθρο 269
Ο ασφαλιστής ενέχεται δι' ας ζημίας το πλοίον, λόγω συγκρούσεως, υποχρεούται έναντι τρίτων, εξαιρέσει των λόγω βλάβης του σώματος ή της υγείας.

Άρθρο 272
Η σύμβασις ασφαλίσεως κατά κοινών θαλασσίων κινδύνων λύεται αφ' ης το πλοίον εκτεθή εις κινδύνους πολεμικούς, εάν δε τούτο συμβή διαρκούντος του πλου, η λύσις επέρχεται άμα των κατάπλω εις τον πρώτο λιμένα.

Άρθρο 274
Ο ασφαλιστής δεν απαλλάσσεται εκ μόνου του γεγονότος ότι αι απώλειαι και αι ζημίαι οφείλονται εις υπαιτιότητα του πλοιάρχου, του πληρώματος ή άλλων προσώπων.

Άρθρο 276
Η ρήτρα «ελεύθερον αβαρίας» απαλλάσσει τον ασφαλιστήν πάσης υποχρεώσεως εκ ζημιών, αι οποίαι δεν συνιστούν ολικήν απώλειαν ή περίπτωσιν εγκαταλείψεως.

Άρθρο 280
Ο ησφαλισμένος δικαιούται να εγκαταλείψει εις τον ασφαλιστήν τα ασφαλισθέντα αντικείμενα και να απαιτήση το οφειλόμενον επί ολικής απωλείας ασφάλισμα, εις τας περιπτώσεις και υπό τους όρους των επομένων άρθρων.

Άρθρο 281
Η εγκατάλειψις του πλοίου ή του φορτίου ή του ναύλου, δύναται να γίνη μόνο όταν α) το πλοίον, συνεπεία θαλασσίου συμβεβηκότος, απωλεσθή ή περιήλθεν εις κατάστασιν ανικανότητος προς πλουν και δεν δύναται να επισκευασθή, β) τα έξοδα δια την ανέλκυσιν, την επισκευήν και την επαναφοράν του βλαβέντος πλοίου εις κατάστασιν επιτρέπουσαν να εξακολουθήση τούτο την ναυσιπλοΐαν, υπερβαίνουν τα τρία τέταρτα της ασφαλιστικής αξίας ή όταν η επισκευή δεν είναι εφικτήεις τον τόπον του ατυχήματος, ουδ' είναι δυνατή η αυτόθι μεταφορά των μέσων της επισκευής ή η ρυμούλκησις του πλοίου εις λιμένα ένθα δύναται να επισκευασθή, γ) από της τελευταίας ειδήσεως περί του πλοίου παρήλθον τουλάχιστον τρεις μήνες προκειμένου περί πλοίων μηχανοκινήτων, προκειμένου δε περί ιστιοφόρων πέντε μήνες, οπότε ο κίνδυνος θεωρείται πραγματοποιηθείς την επομένην της ημέρας εις ην ανάγεται η τελευταία είδησις και δ) το πλοίον αλωθή ή εμποδισθή κατά διαταγήν ξένης δυνάμεως, η δε ασφάλισις καλύπτει τους κινδύνους πολέμου.

Άρθρο 282
Εις την περίπτωσιν δ' του προηγουμένου άρθρου το προς εγκατάλειψιν δικαίωμα δεν δύναται ν' ασκηθή πριν ή παρέλθη τρίμηνον από της γνωστοποιήσεως της αλώσεως ή της εμποδίσεως.

Άρθρο 283

Το προς εγκατάλειψιν δικαίωμα ασκείται εντός προθεσμίας τριών μηνών, αρχομένης την επιούσαν της ημέρας καθ' ην εγένετο γνωστόν το ατύχημα ή της ημέρας, καθ' ην συνεπληρώθη η κατά το άρθρον 281 περίπτωσις γ' ή κατά το άρθρον 282 προθεσμία.

Άρθρο 284

Το προς εγκατάλειψιν δικαίωμα ασκείται δια δηλώσεως κοινοποιουμένης προς τον ασφαλιστήν.

Άρθρο 285

Εάν ο ασφαλιστής, εντός τριάκοντα ημερών από της κοινοποιήσεως της δηλώσεως περί εγκαταλείψεως, δεν αμφισβητήση το δικαίωμα της εγκαταλείψεως ή εάν τούτο αναγνωρισθή δικαστικώς, τα επί των εγκαταλειπομένων αντικειμένων δικαιώματα μεταβιβάζονται εις τον ασφαλιστήν. Η μεταβίβασις θεωρείται συντελεσθείσα από της κοινοποιήσεως της περί εγκαταλείψεως δηλώσεως.
Ο ησφαλισμένος υποχρεούται να παράσχη εις τον ασφαλιστήν τας υπαρχούσας πληροφορίας και να παραδώση εις αυτόν τα εις την κατοχήν του αποδεικτικά έγγραφα.

Άρθρο 287

Ο ασφαλιστής δύναται, δια δηλώσεως κοινοποιουμένης εις τον ησφαλισμένον αμελλητί, να αποποιηθή την κτήσιν της κυριότητος επί του εγκαταλειφθέντος, προσφερόμενος συγχρόνως ανεπιφυλάκτως εις την καταβολήν του όλου ασφαλίσματος.

Άρθρο 288

Ο ασφαλιστής δικαιούται να προκαλέση τον ησφαλισμένον όπως προβή εις εγκατάλειψιν εντός ευλόγου, υπ' αυτού τασσομένης προθεσμίας. Παρελθούσης δε ταύτης απράκτου, ο ησφαλισμένος στερείται του δικαιώματος της εγκαταλείψεως.

APPENDIX III
THE HELLENIC CODE OF PRIVATE MARITIME LAW
(ENGLISH TRANSLATION)

First Title
About Ships and Ship-owners
Article 1
Ship, for the purposes of the present law, is every vessel of a minimum net ten tonnage purported to move independently in the sea.
The provisions of the third, fourth, sixth, seventh, twelfth, thirteenth and fourteenth titles of the present law apply by analogy also to every other navigable structure.

Twelfth Title
About Collision between Vessels

Article 235
In vessels collision, if that happen because of an accidental fact or *force majeure* or if there is doubt about its causes, the damages burden the parties who suffered them.

Article 236
If the collision caused by fault of one of the ships the damages burden the fault ship.
In case of common fault each ship is liable in analogy of the degree of its fault. If it is not possible to define the analogy or if there is equal fault, the liability is split into two equal parts.

Article 245
The provisions of the present title apply also to collision of ships even anchored.

Fourteenth Title
About Marine Insurance

Article 269
The insurer is liable for those damages that the ship, because of a collision, owes to third parties, except for those damages caused against body or health.

Article 272
The insurance contract against common marine perils is terminated if the ship is exposed to war risks, and if that happens during the voyage, the termination occurs when the ship enters into the first port.

Article 274
The insurer is not released from liability on the only fact that the losses and damages have been caused by the captain, the crew or other persons.

Article 276
The term "average free" releases the insurer from any liability for damages which do not constitute total loss or an abandonment case.

Article 280
The assured has the right to abandon to the underwriter the subject – matter insured and to claim for a total loss, in the cases and under the conditions of the following articles.

Article 281
The abandonment of the vessel or the cargo or the freight, may be exercised only when a) the ship, in consequence of a maritime casualty, is lost or is no more capable of navigation and any repair of it is not possible, b) the cost of refloating, repairing and restoration of the ship in a condition where it may continue navigating, exceed three – fourths of the insured value or when the repair is not attainable on the place of the casualty, nor is it possible the transportation of the repair means thereon or the towage of the ship to port where it may be repaired, γ) (c)) from the last news for the ship three months have passed for machine – operated ships, or five months for sailing ships, therefore the peril is considered to have occurred the day following the day when the last news was heard and δ) (d)) the ship is captured or detained (hindered) by order of foreign power, and the insurance policy cover the war risks.

Article 282
In case d (δ) of the previous article the right to abandonment shall not be exercised before the lapse of three months after the notice of the capture or detainment.

Article 283
The right to abandonment is exercised within a time – limit of three months, which starts running the next day of the day when the casualty became known or the day when the time – limit of article 281 (c) or of article 282 has been completed.

Article 284
The right to abandonment is exercised by declaration notified to the insurer.

Article 285

If the insurer, within thirty days after the notification of the declaration of abandonment, does not raise doubts for the right to abandonment or if the right to abandonment is judicially acknowledged (recognised), the rights upon the remaining objects are transferred to the insurer. The transfer of the ownership is considered to have occurred immediately after the notification of the declaration of abandonment.

The assured is obligated to provide the insurer with all the existing information and to dispatch to the insurer the documents and the evidence that the assured possesses.

Article 287

The insurer may, by declaration notified to the assured immediately (after the notified declaration of abandonment), reject his right to ownership upon the abandoned subject – matter, indemnifying unconditionally the assured for a total loss.

Article 288

The underwriter has the right to set for the assured a specific and reasonable time – limit within which the assured may notify his declaration of abandonment. If such time – limit passes, the assured is deprived of the right to abandonment.

APPENDIX IV
INSTITUTE TIME CLAUSES FREIGHT
1/11/95

7
Perils
7.1 This insurance covers loss of the subject-matter insured caused by
7.1.1. perils of the seas rivers lakes or other navigable waters
7.1.2. fire, explosion
7.1.4 jettison
7.1.5 piracy
7.1.6 contact with land conveyance, dock or harbour equipment or installation
7.2 This insurance covers loss of the subject-matter insured caused by
7.2.4 barratry of Master Officers or Crew
7.2.5. contact with aircraft, helicopters or similar objects, or objects falling therefrom
provided that such loss or damage has not resulted from want of due diligence by the Assured, Owners, Managers or Superintendents or any of their onshore management.

The following clauses shall be paramount and shall override anything contained in this insurance inconsistent therewith.

18
War exclusion
In no case shall this insurance cover loss damage liability or expense caused by
18.1 war civil war revolution rebellion insurrection, or civil strife arising therefrom, or any hostile act by or against a belligerent power
18.2 capture seizure arrest restraint or detainment (barratry and piracy excepted), and the consequences thereof or any attempt thereat
18.3 derelict mines torpedoes bombs or other derelict weapons of war.

19
Strikes exclusion
In no case shall this insurance cover loss damage liability or expense caused by
19.1 strikers, locked-out workmen, or persons taking part in labour disturbances, riots or civil commotions
19.2 any terrorist or any person acting from a political motive.

20
Malicious acts exclusion
In no case shall this insurance cover loss damage liability or expense arising from
20.1 the detonation of an explosive

20.2 any weapon of war and caused by any person acting maliciously or from a political motive.

21

Radioactive contamination exclusion clause

In no case shall this insurance cover loss damage liability or expense directly or indirectly caused by or contributed to by or arising from

21.1 ionising radiations

21.2 the radioactive, toxic, explosive or other hazardous or contaminating properties of any nuclear installation

21.3 any weapon of war employing atomic or nuclear fission and / or fusion or other like reaction or radioactive force or matter.

Appendix V
Institute Time Clauses Hulls
1/11/95

6

Perils

6.1 This insurance covers loss of or damage to the subject-matter insured caused by

6.1.1. perils of the seas rivers lakes or other navigable waters

6.1.2. fire, explosion

6.1.6 jettison

6.1.5 piracy

6.1.6 contact with land conveyance, dock or harbour equipment or installation

6.2 This insurance covers loss of or damage to the subject-matter insured caused by

6.2.6 barratry of Master Officers or Crew

6.2.5. contact with aircraft, helicopters or similar objects, or objects falling therefrom

provided that such loss or damage has not resulted from want of due diligence by the Assured, Owners, Managers or Superintendents or any of their onshore management.

8

3/4ths collision liability

8.1 The Underwriters agree to indemnify the Assured for three-fourths of any sum or sums paid by the Assured to any other person or persons by reason of the Assured becoming legally liable by way of damages for

8.1.1 loss of or damage to any other vessel or property thereon.

9

Sistership

Should the Vessel hereby insured come into collision with or receive salvage services from another vessel belonging wholly or in part to the same Owners or under the same management, the Assured shall have the same rights under this insurance as they would have were the other vessel entirely the property of Owners not interested in the Vessel hereby insured; but in such cases the liability for the collision or the amount payable for the services rendered shall be referred to a sole arbitrator to be agreed upon between the Underwriters and the Assured.

The following clauses shall be paramount and shall override anything contained in this insurance inconsistent therewith.

24
War exclusion
In no case shall this insurance cover loss damage liability or expense caused by
24.1 war civil war revolution rebellion insurrection, or civil strife arising therefrom, or any hostile act by or against a belligerent power
24.2 capture seizure arrest restraint or detainment (barratry and piracy excepted), and the consequences thereof or any attempt thereat
24.3 derelict mines torpedoes bombs or other derelict weapons of war.

25
Strikes exclusion
In no case shall this insurance cover loss damage liability or expense caused by
25.1 strikers, locked-out workmen, or persons taking part in labour disturbances, riots or civil commotions
25.2 any terrorist or any person acting from a political motive.

26
Malicious acts exclusion
In no case shall this insurance cover loss damage liability or expense arising from
26.1 the detonation of an explosive
26.2 any weapon of war and caused by any person acting maliciously or from a political motive.

27
Radioactive contamination exclusion clause
In no case shall this insurance cover loss damage liability or expense directly or indirectly caused by or contributed to by or arising from
27.1 ionising radiations
27.2 the radioactive, toxic, explosive or other hazardous or contaminating properties of any nuclear installation
27.3 any weapon of war employing atomic or nuclear fission and / or fusion or other like reaction or radioactive force or matter.

APPENDIX VI
INSTITUTE VOYAGE CLAUSES FREIGHT
1/11/95

4

Perils

4.1 This insurance covers loss of or damage to the subject-matter insured caused by

4.1.1. perils of the seas rivers lakes or other navigable waters

4.1.2. fire, explosion

4.1.4 jettison

4.1.5 piracy

4.1.6 contact with land conveyance, dock or harbour equipment or installation

4.2 This insurance covers loss of or damage to the subject-matter insured caused by

4.2.4 barratry of Master Officers or Crew

4.2.5. contact with aircraft, helicopters or similar objects, or objects falling therefrom

provided that such loss or damage has not resulted from want of due diligence by the Assured, Owners, Managers or Superintendents or any of their onshore management.

7

Sistership

Should the Vessel hereby insured come into collision with or receive salvage services from another vessel belonging wholly or in part to the same Owners or under the same management, the Assured shall have the same rights under this insurance as they would have were the other vessel entirely the property of Owners not interested in the Vessel named herein; but in such cases the liability for the collision or the amount payable for the services rendered shall be referred to a sole arbitrator to be agreed upon between the Underwriters and the Assured.

The following clauses shall be paramount and shall override anything contained in this insurance inconsistent therewith.

14

War exclusion

In no case shall this insurance cover loss damage liability or expense caused by

14.1 war civil war revolution rebellion insurrection, or civil strife arising therefrom, or any hostile act by or against a belligerent power

14.2 capture seizure arrest restraint or detainment (barratry and piracy excepted), and the consequences thereof or any attempt thereat

14.3 derelict mines torpedoes bombs or other derelict weapons of war.

15

Strikes exclusion

In no case shall this insurance cover loss damage liability or expense caused by

15.1 strikers, locked-out workmen, or persons taking part in labour disturbances, riots or civil commotions

15.2 any terrorist or any person acting from a political motive.

16

Malicious acts exclusion

In no case shall this insurance cover loss damage liability or expense arising from

16.1 the detonation of an explosive

16.2 any weapon of war and caused by any person acting maliciously or from a political motive.

17

Radioactive contamination exclusion clause

In no case shall this insurance cover loss damage liability or expense directly or indirectly caused by or contributed to by or arising from

17.1 ionising radiations

17.2 the radioactive, toxic, explosive or other hazardous or contaminating properties of any nuclear installation

17.3 any weapon of war employing atomic or nuclear fission and / or fusion or other like reaction or radioactive force or matter.

Appendix VII
Institute Voyage Clauses Hulls
1/11/95

4

Perils

4.1 This insurance covers loss of or damage to the subject-matter insured caused by

4.1.1. perils of the seas rivers lakes or other navigable waters

4.1.2. fire, explosion

4.1.4 jettison

4.1.5 piracy

4.1.6 contact with land conveyance, dock or harbour equipment or installation

4.2 This insurance covers loss of or damage to the subject-matter insured caused by

4.2.4 barratry of Master Officers or Crew

4.2.5. contact with aircraft, helicopters or similar objects, or objects falling therefrom

provided that such loss or damage has not resulted from want of due diligence by the Assured, Owners, Managers or Superintendents or any of their onshore management.

6

3/4ths collision liability

6.1 The Underwriters agree to indemnify the Assured for three-fourths of any sum or sums paid by the Assured to any other person or persons by reason of the Assured becoming legally liable by way of damages for

6.1.1 loss of or damage to any other vessel or property thereon.

7

Sistership

Should the Vessel hereby insured come into collision with or receive salvage services from another vessel belonging wholly or in part to the same Owners or under the same management, the Assured shall have the same rights under this insurance as they would have were the other vessel entirely the property of Owners not interested in the Vessel thereby insured, but in such cases the liability for the collision or the amount payable for the services rendered shall be referred to a sole arbitrator to be agreed upon between the Underwriters and the Assured.

11

Notice of claim and tenders

11.1 In the event of accident whereby loss or damage may result in a claim under this insurance, notice must be given to the Underwriters promptly after the date on which the Assured, Owners or Managers become or should have become aware of the loss or damage.

17
Constructive total loss
17.1 In ascertaining whether the Vessel is a constructive total loss, the insured value shall be taken as the repaired value and nothing in respect of the damaged or break-up value of the Vessel or wreck shall be taken into account.

The following clauses shall be paramount and shall override anything contained in this insurance inconsistent therewith.

21
War exclusion
In no case shall this insurance cover loss damage liability or expense caused by
21.1 war civil war revolution rebellion insurrection, or civil strife arising therefrom, or any hostile act by or against a belligerent power
21.2 capture seizure arrest restraint or detainment (barratry and piracy excepted), and the consequences thereof or any attempt thereat
21.3 derelict mines torpedoes bombs or other derelict weapons of war.

22
Strikes exclusion
In no case shall this insurance cover loss damage liability or expense caused by
22.1 strikers, locked-out workmen, or persons taking part in labour disturbances, riots or civil commotions
22.2 any terrorist or any person acting from a political motive.

23
Malicious acts exclusion
In no case shall this insurance cover loss damage liability or expense arising from
23.1 the detonation of an explosive
23.2 any weapon of war and caused by any person acting maliciously or from a political motive.

24
Radioactive contamination exclusion clause
In no case shall this insurance cover loss damage liability or expense directly or indirectly caused by or contributed to by or arising from
24.1 ionising radiations
24.2 the radioactive, toxic, explosive or other hazardous or contaminating properties of any nuclear installation

24.3 any weapon of war employing atomic or nuclear fission and / or fusion or other like reaction or radioactive force or matter.

APPENDIX VIII
BÜRGERLICHES GESETZBUCH

§ 318
(2) Die Anfechtung der getroffenen Bestimmung wegen Irrtums, Drohung oder arglistiger Täuschung steht [..] den Vertragschliessenden zu; Anfechtungsgegner ist der andere Teil. Die Anfechtung muss unverzüglich erfolgen, nachdem der Anfechtungsberechtigte von dem Anfechtungsgrund Kenntnis erlangt hat. Sie ist ausgeschlossen, wenn 30 Jahre verstrichen sind, nachdem die Bestimmung getroffen worden ist.

APPENDIX IX
STRAFGESETZBUCH

§ 263
(1) Wer in der Absicht, sich oder einem Dritten einen rechtswidrigen Vermögensvorteil zu verschaffen, das Vermögen eines anderen dadurch beschädigt, dass er durch Vorspiegelung falscher oder durch Entstellung oder Unterdrückung wahrer Tatsachen einen Irrtum erregt oder unterhält, wird mit Freiheitsstrafe bis zu fünf Jahren oder mit Geldstrafe bestraft [Betrug].

APPENDIX X
THE HELLENIC CIVIL CODE (ENGLISH TRANSLATION)

Article 173
In interpreting the unilateral contractual statement the true will shall be sought without only staying in the letter.

Article 200
The contracts are interpreted on the basis of good faith, taking into account of the contractual morals.

Article 281
The exercise of a right is forbidden if it obviously goes beyond the limits which are set by the good faith or the morals or the social or the economic goal of that right.

Index

Numbers refer to pages

Peter Lang · Europäischer Verlag der Wissenschaften

Johan Hendrik Botes

From Good Faith to Utmost Good Faith in Marine Insurance

Frankfurt am Main, Berlin, Bern, Bruxelles, New York, Oxford, Wien, 2006.
239 pp.
ISBN 978-3-631-55549-1 · pb. € 42.50*

Apart from its geographical import, the English Channel is also of legal importance serving as the divide between two distinct legal traditions. The sea, being the manifestation of this border, is also the symbolic arena for one of the most contentious modern distinctions between the Civilian and Common Law traditions, namely between good faith and utmost good faith in marine insurance. In essence this work is a critique of the English principle of utmost good faith. The author places *Carter v Boehm* in its Civilian context. The book includes a comprehensive collection of texts by Civilian writers on the topic of good faith in marine insurance in both the original version and translation.

Contents: The history of the marine insurance contract · The history of good faith in marine insurance law · Good faith and the marine insurance contract on the Continent · The history of the principle of utmost good faith in marine insurance · The modern principle of utmost good faith · Conclusion: In the matter between good faith and utmost good faith

Frankfurt am Main · Berlin · Bern · Bruxelles · New York · Oxford · Wien
Distribution: Verlag Peter Lang AG
Moosstr. 1, CH-2542 Pieterlen
Telefax 00 41 (0) 32 / 376 17 27

*The €-price includes German tax rate
Prices are subject to change without notice

Homepage http://www.peterlang.de

FSC
www.fsc.org
MIX
Papier | Fördert
gute Waldnutzung
FSC® C083411

Kolibri 360 GmbH
Ferdinand-Jühlke-Straße 7
99095 Erfurt, Deutschland
produktsicherheit@kolibri360.de

Druck:
CPI Druckdienstleistungen GmbH
im Auftrag der
Kolibri 360 GmbH
Ferdinand-Jühlke-Str. 7
99095 Erfurt